The History of Alternative Rock

Stuart A. Kallen

LUCENT BOOKS

A part of Gale, Cengage Learning

GALE
CENGAGE Learning™

Detroit • New York • San Francisco • New Haven, Conn • Waterville, Maine • London

LIBRARY OF CONGRESS CATALOGING-IN-PUBLICATION DATA

Kallen, Stuart A., 1955-
   The history of alternative rock / by Stuart A. Kallen.
     p. cm. -- (The music library)
   Includes bibliographical references and index.
   ISBN 978-1-4205-0738-6 (hardcover)
  1. Alternative rock music--History and criticism--Juvenile literature. I. Title.
   ML3534.K32 2012
    781.6609--dc23   2011047271

Lucent Books
27500 Drake Rd
Farmington Hills MI 48331

ISBN-13: 978-1-4205-0738-6
ISBN-10: 1-4205-0738-9

Printed in the United States of America
2 3 4 5 6 7 16 15 14 13 12

CONTENTS

In the nineteenth century, English novelist Charles Kingsley wrote, "Music speaks straight to our hearts and spirits, to the very core and root of our souls. . . . Music soothes us, stirs us up . . . melts us to tears." As Kingsley stated, music is much more than just a pleasant arrangement of sounds. It is the resonance of emotion, a joyful noise, a human endeavor that can soothe the spirit or excite the soul. Musicians can also imitate the expressive palette of the earth, from the violent fury of a hurricane to the gentle flow of a babbling brook.

The word *music* is derived from the fabled Greek muses, the children of Apollo who ruled the realms of inspiration and imagination. Composers have long called upon the muses for help and insight. Music is not merely the result of emotions and pleasurable sensations, however.

Music is a discipline subject to formal study and analysis. It involves the juxtaposition of creative elements such as rhythm, melody, and harmony with intellectual aspects of composition, theory, and instrumentation. Like painters mixing red, blue, and yellow into thousands of colors, musicians blend these various elements to create classical symphonies, jazz improvisations, country ballads, and rock-and-roll tunes.

Throughout centuries of musical history, individual musical elements have been blended and modified in infinite ways. The resulting sounds may convey a whole range of moods, emotions, reactions, and messages. Music, then, is both an expression and reflection of human experience and emotion.

The foundations of modern musical styles were laid down by the first ancient musicians who used wood, rocks, animal skins—and their own bodies—to re-create the sounds of the natural world in which they lived. With their hands, their feet, and their very breath they ignited the passions of listeners and moved them to their feet. The dancing, in turn, had a mesmerizing and hypnotic effect that allowed people to transcend their worldly concerns. Through music they could achieve a level of shared experience that could not be found in other forms of communication. For this reason, music has always been part of religious endeavors, from ancient Egyptian spiritual ceremonies to modern Christian masses. And it has inspired dance movements from kings and queens spinning the minuet to punk rockers slamming together in a mosh pit.

By examining musical genres ranging from Western classical music to rock and roll, readers will find a new understanding of old music and develop an appreciation for new sounds. Books in Lucent's Music Library focus on the music, the musicians, the instruments, and on music's place in cultural history. The songs and artists examined may be easily found in the CD and sheet music collections of local libraries so that readers may study and enjoy the music covered in the books. Informative sidebars, annotated bibliographies, and complete indexes highlight the text in each volume and provide young readers with many opportunities for further discussion and research.

Indies, Phonies, and Alts

Alternative rock is a style of music that has been evolving since the 1980s among bands utilizing a standard rock-and-roll format—guitars, bass, drums, and keyboards. Alt-rock has always differed from the straight-ahead, sing-along music by mainstream superstar acts like Michael Jackson, Madonna, Britney Spears, and Taylor Swift. Rather than make music for broad commercial appeal, alt-rockers draw from a variety of styles not considered consumer friendly. Over the years, alt-rock has tapped into garage rock, punk, new wave, rap, thrash, hard core, and countless mash ups of these genres.

The new breed of alternative musicians not only created a new sound, but also put forth a different attitude. Alt-rockers value independence, experimentation, and truth-telling. In the early days of alternative, or indie, rock, the players outwardly rejected the musical standards and sales practices set by major record companies.

Before the Internet, computer compact disc (CD) burners, and iPods made sharing music ubiquitous and influential, popular musical tastes were chiefly dictated by executives working for huge entertainment conglomerates. During the 1980s, record companies signed musical acts they thought would appeal to the largest group of consumers and thus generate the most money. Approved bands recorded their albums in expensive, exclusive studios. The final product, whether vinyl, tape, or CD, was sold at record store chains, most of which were also owned by large entertainment companies.

Major music labels worked closely with radio and cable TV executives to ensure airtime for their artists' music. Powerful radio show programmers picked the music that would be played on the air in every city in the country. Cable producers handpicked music videos that would be viewed on channels MTV and VH1 by tens of millions of viewers. Both venues, in turn, generated billions of dollars in record sales. The majority of people who made these decisions were not musicians or artists, but rather businessmen—and a few businesswomen. To them, music was product, and bands that did not meet predetermined sales figures were quickly dropped.

Creative Risks

Record companies operated in their self-contained, exclusive environment for decades while making huge profits. As a result, creators of alternative music in the 1980s had to develop their own systems to survive. They performed in local bars and cafés where like-minded individuals valued music that was quirky, creative, and free of pretension. Bands relied on their local fans to bring friends to gigs, and for some, fame spread by word of mouth.

Alternative bands appealed to new listeners through photocopied fan magazines, or fanzines, that might have had fifty or five hundred readers. Indie acts also relied on tapers who recorded live performances and traded the music among themselves. A group that built a big enough fan base in a local music scene could hope to sign with a small independent, or indie, record label and possibly sell a few thousand CDs.

College Radio

Commercial radio programmers would not play new or innovative alt-rock bands. As a result, college FM radio

U2, the most famous alternative rock band in the world, performs on The Tube, *a British TV show, in 1983.*

stations, along with a few independent listener-supported community stations, became havens for alternative rock by the late 1980s. Staffed by volunteers, most of the stations were low-powered and could only be heard within a few miles of the college. Despite their limited reach, these stations became very influential. College disc jockeys (DJs) are credited with inventing the term *alternative* to describe unconventional styles of music. Some of the most successful alternative rock bands, such as U2, R.E.M., and Nirvana, owe their initial success to college radio.

By relying on low-watt radio stations, fanzines, and dedicated fans, the mosaic of alternative, alt, or indie culture was generated by band after band in town after town. According to indie music journalist Kaya Oakes, people in the early indie culture worked together to cultivate many positive things: "credibility, freedom, the ability to promote their own work and control how it's promoted, self-reliance, open-mindedness, and the freedom to take creative risks."[1]

All-Too-Familiar Bands

Credibility, freedom, and creative risks still defined alternative music in the early 1990s, but technology changed the alternative rock scene. The World Wide Web, which went online in 1993, provided a burgeoning forum for alternative culture and a new way for musicians to promote themselves. Bands created websites to provide access to their music and gig schedules, while their fans also took advantage of the new media. Countless alt-music websites, blogs, and newsgroups sprang into existence and provided a community for like-minded individuals to share music and, oftentimes, engage in acrimonious debates over a band's worth.

Today, people in alternative rock culture continue to shun mainstream music, favoring less commercial acts. However, even the most obscure acts can become nationally famous overnight when promoted on a popular alternative music website like Pitchfork. This makes the group mainstream, and therefore no longer alternative. As Bill Wasik, senior editor of *Harper's*, explains, "Facebook, iTunes, and Internet radio make location and friends irrelevant for discovering music. Blogs and aggregators [information-gathering organizations] enable fans to determine in just a few minutes what everyone else is listening to that day. What you know, where you are—these matter not at all. To be an insider today one must merely be fast. . . . Unknown bands become all-too-familiar bands in a month, and abandoned bands the next month."[2]

The Worst Crime

The debate over mainstream music versus alternative rock goes back several decades. Before his death in 1994, Kurt Cobain, singer, songwriter, and guitarist for the grunge band Nirvana, wrote, "The worst crime is faking it."[3] Perhaps this short sentence best sums up the attitude of alternative rockers. Whatever musical genres they play, independent musicians are opposed to music that is contrived, clichéd, and performed by those they perceive as phonies.

Most alt-rock musicians want to believe their music is sincere, addressing real emotions and played from the heart.

People have longed for authenticity in music for decades. Whether it is provided by flippant punk rockers Green Day, morose grunge rockers Nirvana, or peppy jangle popsters Vampire Weekend, the music is an authentic alternative to commercial pop. For those who take their music seriously, alternative rock continues to grow and change, regenerating, re-creating, and producing fresh new sounds for every mood and every new day of the year.

CHAPTER 1

Garage Rockers and Proto-Punks

I n 1989, *New York Times* music critic Jon Pareles wrote about an innovative sound that was sweeping the nation:

On the fringe of mainstream rock, a new style is coalescing [coming together]. The loose network of college . . . radio stations, rock-club disk jockeys and active music fans . . . has nurtured an 'alternative rock' that's more melodic than post-punk hard-core rock yet looser, more unruly and less formulaic than big-budget [popular rock groups] such as Bon Jovi. In a few years, alternative rock (probably with a better name) is likely to be just one more commercial genre, but for the moment rock [musicians] share it with misfits, idealists and other do-it-yourselfers.[4]

Pareles was alerted to what he called "a new kind of rock" by the mainstream success of the alternative rock band R.E.M. The group, from Athens, Georgia, typified alternative rock bands of the era. R.E.M. formed in a smallish college town where it attracted a loyal following. The band first became a regional success and signed with a small, independent record label. Like those of other alternative bands, R.E.M.'s members rejected most commercial pop rock played on radio and MTV. They believed music on Top 40 radio was played by phonies—poseurs who lacked integrity.

Despite R.E.M.'s rejection of the musical marketplace, after seven years on the indie rock scene, the group scored a major hit with the 1987 song "It's the End of the World As We Know It (And I Feel Fine)." In the aftermath, R.E.M. was as popular as any other group on Top 40 radio or MTV.

Like other successful alternative rock bands, R.E.M. wrote songs with memorable choruses and catchy musical passages, called hooks. Pareles linked them to alternative music culture because R.E.M echoed "regular-guy voices . . . proclaiming cynicism, confusion, hostility, self-mockery, disillusionment and sardonic humor, along with hints of well-guarded sincerity."[5]

"An Act of God"

Jon Pareles hoped alternative rock would get a better name, but it never did, although it is also called alt-rock and indie rock. Whatever it is called, alternative rock embodies elements of about a dozen musical genres—including punk, new wave, heavy metal, and grunge—that emerged between 1975 and the early 1990s. Alt-rock was also influenced by rock and roll produced in the 1960s. The songs of the sixties acted as prototypes, influencing musicians decades after they were written. *Proto* means earliest or first, and certain songs from the 1960s have been labeled proto-punk, proto-grunge, or proto-alternative.

The influential music critics Dave Marsh and Greil Marcus believe that virtually all punk rock can be traced back to a single proto-punk song, "Louie Louie." It was recorded in 1963 by the Kingsmen, a quintet from Portland, Oregon.

Almost everyone is familiar with the Kingsmen's version of "Louie Louie." It has been played by countless high school marching bands during halftime at football games. The song has also been played or recorded by dozens of famous—and infamous—musical acts, among them the surf rockers the Beach Boys, new wavers Blondie, rock composer Frank Zappa, punk pioneers Iggy and the Stooges, hard-core punkers Black Flag, heavy metal maniacs Motorhead, jazz bassist Stanley Clarke, soul singer Otis Redding, the reggae group

Toots and the Maytals, alt-rockers the Smashing Pumpkins, and rock superstar Bruce Springsteen.

The influence of "Louie Louie" can be heard in dozens of best-selling songs recorded since it was released half a century ago. Songs based on the chord pattern of "Louie Louie" include "Get Off of My Cloud" by the Rolling Stones, "Purple Haze" by Jimi Hendrix, and "Smells Like Teen Spirit" by Nirvana. Rock critic Marsh explains how the song transformed over the years: "["Louie Louie" was] a joke in the late Sixties, when bands like [Frank Zappa's] Mothers of Invention would play it to make fun of the old fashioned rock 'n' roll they had transcended; by the late Seventies and in the Eighties the tune was all pervasive, like a law of nature or an act of God."[6]

"Slurred and Unintelligible Vocals"

"Louie Louie" was composed by African American singer and songwriter Richard Berry in 1956. It was originally written as a rhythm and blues (R&B) style doo-wop song sung with sweet vocal harmonies. The lyrics tell the story of a Jamaican sailor returning home to his girlfriend. Berry's original recording of "Louie Louie" was unsuccessful, selling

The Kingsmen's version of "Louie, Louie" recorded in 1963 exemplified the raw rock sound of later garage rockers.

only forty thousand copies. The song took on a new life when the Kingsmen entered a Portland sound studio and recorded it in one take, releasing it complete with mistakes in the summer of 1963.

Members of the Kingsmen were still in their teens when they made "Louie Louie." Eighteen-year-old guitarist and vocalist Jack Ely was the oldest member of the Kingsmen. Fifteen-year-old electric piano player Don Gallucci was the youngest. All of the band members, except one, lived at home with his parents. The Kingsmen might not have been the first garage rockers, but "Louie Louie" certainly exemplified the raw rock sound that came to be identified with the style.

The term *garage rock* originated as a dismissive insult, a label applied to music made by young, amateurish musicians who practiced in their parents' suburban garages or basements. Garage rockers play songs based on a few repetitive guitar chords, simple bass lines, and sharp snare drumbeats. They are often sung by gravel-voiced vocalists who can barely carry a tune. On the liner notes to the 1991 CD *The Best of the Kingsmen*, Seattle, Washington, rock historian Peter Blecha perfectly describes the garage rock sound, referring to the "Kingsmen's chaotic version [of "Louie Louie"]—with its clubfooted drum beat, insane cymbal crashes, ultra-cheezy keyboard figures, lead guitar spazzout/solo, and that famous fluffed third verse, as well as Ely's generally slurred and unintelligible vocals."[7]

Panicking Authority Figures

While the drumming was inept and piano pounding less than stellar, it was Jack Ely's incoherent vocals that helped make "Louie Louie" a worldwide hit. After the first line, the words to the song are virtually unintelligible. This gave rise to the myth that Ely was singing obscene lyrics. The urban legend, which has no identifiable source, states that if a listener played the 45 rpm (revolutions per minute) single of "Louie Louie" on a record player at 33 rpm, the slower speed would reveal dirty words. As Dave Marsh writes, "The preposterous fable bore no scrutiny even at the time, but kids

The Gospel of "Louie Louie"

Dave Marsh, associate editor of Rolling Stone, *wrote an entire book about the influence of the Richard Berry song "Louie Louie." In what he calls the "Gospel of Louie Louie," Marsh describes how the song spawned punk rock:*

Now it came to pass in the fullness of time that "Louie Louie" begat all that was Mod with the British beat. "You Really Got Me" [by the Kinks], "I Can't Explain" [the Who], "All Day and All of the Night" [the Kinks], "My Generation" [the Who], all these "Louie Louie" begat. And "My Generation" [the Who] in unison with frat rock begat "Wild Thing" [Troggs], "Gloria" [Them], "She's About a Mover" [Sir Douglas Quintet], "Wooly Bully" [Sam the Sham and the Pharaohs], "Double Shot (of My Baby's Love)" [Swingin' Medallions]—yea, even unto "Purple Haze" [Jimi Hendrix Experience] did it beget the unholy ructions of rock 'n' roll.

And "Purple Haze" begat many deformed spawn . . . "I Wanna Be Your Dog" [the Stooges] which begat the New York Dolls. And the New York Dolls begat the Ramones, and Ramones and the New York Dolls begat the Sex Pistols of "Anarchy in the U.K." and the Clash of "Clash City Rockers." And in those days punks walked the earth.

Dave Marsh. *Louie Louie*. New York: Hyperion, 1993, p. 139.

used to pretend that it did, in order to panic parents, teachers, and authority figures."[8]

It may be hard for someone in the twenty-first century to imagine how controversial any hint of "dirty" lyrics might have been in 1963. During this era, before the Beatles arrived in the United States, number-one hit songs on the music charts were mostly bland, innocent teen pop ditties like

"Blue Velvet" by crooner Bobby Vinton and "Dominique" by the Singing Nuns—four French nuns who lived in a monastery. In this more innocent time, rumors of the filthy lyrics in "Louie Louie" reached the highest levels of the federal government.

In late 1963, the Federal Bureau of Investigation (FBI) conducted a thirty-month investigation in six cities to determine if the record producers violated federal law by shipping pornography over state lines. The FBI investigation resulted in an official report that stated "the record . . . was played at various speeds but none of the speeds assisted in determining the words of the song on the record."[9] The controversy drove the song to the top of the charts, and more than 7 million people purchased "Louie Louie," some just to hear the (nonexistent) dirty words for themselves.

The British Invasion

Many famous 1960s garage rock bands were one-hit wonders. This term is applied to groups that have only one chart-topping hit before fading into obscurity. The Kingsmen have the distinction of being one-hit wonders not only in America, but in the United Kingdom (U.K.). "Louie Louie" hit number nine on the U.K. charts on February 4, 1964. As it happened, the English group the Beatles made their first trip to the United States five days later to play on television's *The Ed Sullivan Show*. They were watched by more than 74 million Americans—about half the population of the United States at the time.

If Americans were listening to "Louie Louie" before the Beatles arrived in the United States, they were not in the aftermath. By April, the Beatles held twelve positions on the *Billboard* Hot 100, including the top five songs, a record that remains unbroken. With songs like "She Loves You," "I Want To Hold Your Hand," and "Can't Buy Me Love," the Beatles could not have been more unlike American garage rockers. The Beatles composed clever songs with complex chord patterns, and their vocal arrangements featured sweet, high harmonies. As musicians, the Beatles were controlled, tight, and professional.

The Beatles helped open doors for other bands from the United Kingdom in what is called the British Invasion. These groups, including the Kinks, the Who, the Rolling Stones, and the Animals, had a rougher sound and more raw energy than the Beatles. All British Invasion groups owed a debt of gratitude to the Kingsmen and their version of "Louie Louie," and the U.K. bands helped make the garage rock sound a permanent part of rock and alternative rock history.

Feedback and Power Chords

The influence of the "Louie Louie" chord progression is obvious on two 1964 hits by the Kinks: "You Really Got Me" and "All Day and All of the Night." The Kinks enhanced these songs with a sound produced through creative destruction. Kinks guitarist Dave Davies carved up the speaker in his low-powered amplifier with a razor blade, which gave the song a distorted fuzz tone in an era before the invention of effect pedals to make that sound on countless records.

The Kinks pioneered the use of power chords and anti-conformist lyrics that would influence the alternative rock scene.

Davies also pioneered the use of power chords, simple, amplified guitar strumming that is found on almost every heavy metal and grunge song. Musicologist Eric James Abbey analyzed Davies' sound and noted that:

> [Dave Davies] became known for this simplistic style of playing music. These types of [power] chords . . . are played in such a way that the sound resolution is clipped at the end, which delivers a strong, harsh sound that was influential to every musician that followed. . . . The importance of the development of fuzz tone distortion and the use of power chords cannot be overlooked within the current [indie] scene.[10]

Kinks songwriter and rhythm guitarist Ray Davies (Dave's brother) composed lyrics that also would influence the alternative rock scene. In songs like "Well Respected Man" (1965) and "Dedicated Follower of Fashion" (1966), Ray's mocking, ironic words reveal his intense dislike of conformists, businessmen, and bland suburban life.

Varieties of Frustration

Like punk rockers in later years, the Kinks often displayed violent behavior towards one another onstage. After band members got into a bloody brawl onstage in Cardiff, Wales, the group was banned from playing in the United States for four years. Unable to enter the country at the height of the British Invasion, the Kinks were denied the American commercial success achieved by groups like the Who.

Early Who hits like 1965's "Can't Explain" and "My Generation" were musically similar to "Louie Louie," but the group took the sound to another level with excellent musicianship and a manic stage presence. In "My Generation," lead singer Roger Daltrey expresses the proto-punk sentiment: I hope I die before I get old. Critic Dave Marsh describes the song:

> "My Generation" sped up the *duh duh duh, duh duh* [rhythm of "Louie Louie"] almost beyond recognition (you can hear the theme clearly stated in John Entwistle's bass solo), surrounding it with the clattering drums and a stuttered Roger Daltrey vocal that de-

notes varieties of frustration including but not limited to the sexual, the socioeconomic, and the existential. At the end of the record, these pent-up emotions boil over and *duh duh duh, duh duh* literally explodes, then rains back down in [lead guitarist Pete] Townshend's infamous concluding feedback extravaganza.[11]

The Who took rock music to a new level with excellent musicianship and a manic stage presence.

When performing live, the Who wrapped up their shows with what was then considered shocking behavior. Daltrey swung the microphone over his head on its long wire like a rodeo rider twirling a lasso. Drummer Keith Moon kicked over and trashed his drum kit. After finishing a furious solo, Townshend often rammed his guitar into his amplifier before smashing the instrument repeatedly on the stage as feedback shrieked and wailed.

The Who initially destroyed their instruments because the violence distinguished them from other bands and attracted crowds to their shows. The practice of smashing equipment became quite common in the punk era, and by the 1990s, grunge bands like Nirvana and Pearl Jam regularly abused their musical equipment for the gratification of cheering fans.

"Cynical, Nasty, Skeptical, Rude"

The Rolling Stones did not destroy their equipment onstage, but the band's primary songwriters, Mick Jagger and Keith Richards, also shaped the *duh duh duh, duh duh* of "Louie Louie" into antagonistic, cynical pop masterpieces. In doing so, the Rolling Stones provided immense influence for a generation of alternative rockers.

The Stones had their first number-one hits in 1965. "(I Can't Get No) Satisfaction" and "Get Off of My Cloud" contain variations of the "Louie Louie" riff. The lyrics of these and other Rolling Stones songs were written at a time when a youth rebellion was brewing. Young people were starting to protest the war in Vietnam, while racial tensions touched off destructive riots in urban neighborhoods across the country. The Rolling Stones decided to address the problems of the era, as Richards explains in his 2010 autobiography, *Life*:

> Our songs were taking on some kind of edge in the lyrics . . . cynical, nasty, skeptical, rude. We seemed to be ahead in this respect at the time. . . . The lyrics and the mood of the songs fitted with the kids' disenchantment with the grown-up world of America, and for a while we seemed to be the only provider, the soundtrack for the rumbling of rebellion, touching those social nerves.[12]

The Stones wrote songs that expressed anger, frustration, and irritation. When playing live, Jagger perfected a strutting, brash, and brazen stage presence that was imitated by countless punk and metal singers in later decades.

In the studio, the Rolling Stones produced an unrehearsed, fresh, and spontaneous sound that Richards calls "the anti-Beatles."[13] Along with the Who, the Rolling Stones laid down the foundations of the modern alt-rock movement. As Eric James Abbey writes: "Contemporary [alt-rock] is greatly influenced by these bands, and . . . looks back to the British Invasion for the structure of [its] sound, appearance and musical approach. [The Stones] champion a sound and attitude that was influential in changing the musical landscape of the world."[14]

Telling the Truth and Making Fun

The Stones and the Who wrote great songs, but Bob Dylan's songs permanently changed the soundscape of the 1960s. Dylan began his career as a singer-songwriter in 1962. In the following decades, he composed more than 450 songs that influenced nearly everyone from the Beatles and Rolling Stones to alternative rockers like Beck.

Dylan introduced new subject matter to pop music, drawing on his own personal feelings to compose lyrics about

Bob Dylan recorded his influential album Highway 61 Revisited *in Columbia Records' New York City studio in 1965.*

politics, philosophy, society, and popular culture. He often expressed his opinions in a withering, judgmental snarl, prompting singer Paul Simon to comment, "[Everything Dylan] sings has two meanings. He's telling you the truth and making fun of you at the same time."[15] The 1965 Dylan song "Subterranean Homesick Blues," with its rattling torrent of humor, irony, and scorn, criticizes cops, teachers, the army, and the American dream. *Rolling Stone* called the song "a proto-rap barrage of one-liners sending up America's mixed up confusion."[16] Other Dylan lyrics, according to critic Jon Pareles, consist of "prophecy and hogwash, morality and absurdism, apocalypse and intimacy. . . . Endlessly layered ironies and . . . moments of unexpected tenderness and rage."[17]

Before Dylan had his first number-one hit as a solo artist, his songs were recorded by others, such as Peter, Paul and Mary and the Byrds. While these acts sang Dylan's "Blowing in the Wind" and "Mister Tambourine Man" with sweet, seamless harmonies, his breakthrough hit, 1965's "Like a Rolling Stone," was anything but harmonious. The song is a jangle of guitars, organ, and piano that lopes along behind Dylan's singsong lyrics that skewer pretty people in high society, two-faced hipsters, and other objects of scorn. At more than six minutes in length, "Like a Rolling Stone" was twice as long as the average Top 40 hit at the time and showed Dylan to be the premier songwriter of the century. As Bono, lead singer for the alternative rock group U2, writes, "["Like a Rolling Stone"] is a black eye of a pop song. The verbal pugilism [boxing] on display here cracks open songwriting for a generation. . . . The tumble of words, images, ire, and spleen on 'Rolling Stone' shape-shifts easily into music forms 10 or 20 years away, like punk, grunge, or hip hop."[18]

America's Dirty Water

When Bob Dylan came along, British Invasion bands had ruled the Top 10 for several years. Dylan helped make American music popular again, and around 1966, garage rockers from the United States created catchy, innovative

Grateful Dead's Garage Rock

Alternative rock is defined by several factors. Alternative bands often combine several styles of music in unusual ways. Alt-rockers reject the pop music marketplace in order to play fresh, original material that does not have obvious commercial potential, and bands' fan bases expand due to word of mouth spread by dedicated followers. If any group could be called the founding fathers of alternative rock, it would be the Grateful Dead. Formed in San Francisco, California, in 1965, the Dead were masters at mixing and melding different musical styles. In the second part of the 1960s, they often played the two-and-a-half-minute rock song "Good Lovin'" as an eighteen-minute jam that included elements of blues, jazz, rock, psychedelic noise, and even country. *Rolling Stone* editor Rob Sheffield describes the energy of Grateful Dead music as having "garage rock drive . . . exploding every which way."

The Grateful Dead always allowed people in the audience to tape their concerts, which often lasted more than three hours. With tapers trading shows and playing them for their friends, the Dead's fan base, called Deadheads, expanded to a point that they were among the top touring acts throughout the 1980s, selling almost as many concert tickets as the Rolling Stones. Despite their success on the stage, the group only had one commercial hit, 1987's "Touch of Grey."

Rob Sheffield. "Reviews," *Rolling Stone*, June 9, 2011, p. 72.

new music that challenged the British for dominance on the rock charts. The sound created by the Americans often featured an irritated young man who was fuming about his lying girlfriend. The lyrics were punctuated by shouts, screams, or derisive laughter. Some of the American garage rockers of the era stuck to the "Louie Louie" *duh duh duh* musical formula, while others incorporated fast-paced chord changes and catchy guitar licks.

The one-hit proto-punk wonders of the 1960s displayed angry attitudes that would become commonplace among alternative rockers in later decades. The Standells' 1966 song "Dirty Water" has a "Louie Louie"-like musical structure, complete with cheesy keyboards. The snarling lyrics about a man who sarcastically proclaims his love for the toxic water flowing in Boston, Massachusetts' Charles River might be among the first to express anger about water pollution. In later decades, "Dirty Water" was played and recorded by a host of punk, indie, and alternative bands, including U2, Dropkick Murphy, and the Dave Matthews Band.

Other American garage rockers sang songs from the viewpoint of a loser, a guy rejected by his girl or by society in general. The bouncy, catchy 1966 hit "Little Girl" by Syndicate of Sound encapsulates this mind-set. The singer addresses the girl who cheated on him and tells her she's not the first, and won't be the last, to step out on him and break his heart. The song was played by alt-pioneers R.E.M. in their early years, and has also been recorded by punks like the Residents and the Dead Boys. Lyrics written from the stance of a social misfit, like Beck's 1993 song "Loser," would be common in alt-rock songs in later decades.

Many of the garage groups around during the second half of the sixties were one-hit wonders, but this did not limit their contribution to the modern scene. As Eric James Abbey writes, "The influence that many of the original Garage bands had on future recordings and musical outlooks is extremely important. Many other musical undergrounds have been influenced and have taken their cues from [these American bands]."[19]

Psychedelic, Psychotic Reactions

The American garage rockers were making music at a time when the United States was experiencing dramatic and unprecedented social change. The hippie movement was in full bloom and millions of young men were growing long hair and beards. Millions of men and women were preaching free love, rejecting traditional religious and social values, and experimenting with marijuana and the psychedelic drug LSD (lysergic acid diethylamide, or acid).

The hippie counterculture movement inspired psychedelic garage rockers to choose inventive—some might say silly—names for their bands. This was the era of rock groups named Strawberry Alarm Clock, the Chocolate Watchband, and the Electric Prunes. Whatever the bands were called,

the musicianship of garage rock improved in the second half of the sixties. Musicians were inspired to capture their mind-blowing drug experience in concert and on record. This led to longer songs, weirder lyrics, and musical experimentation that included heavy drums and more intricate guitar licks and bass lines.

The Blues Magoos' 1966 hit "(We Ain't Got) Nothin' Yet" is an example of the new psychedelic garage sound. The song features a rocking bass drum, a rolling bass line, and an echo-heavy exhilarating guitar line that ascends to the stratosphere. The hit single was included on the memorably named Blues Magoos album *Psychedelic Lollipop*, the first record to use the term *psychedelic*.

While the Blues Magoos were one-hit wonders, the San Francisco, California-based Grateful Dead had a nearly thirty-year career playing psychedelic music. Formed in 1965, the group rose to fame promoted not by a record company, but by a grassroots network of fans called Deadheads.

Jerry Garcia, left, and Bob Weir of the Grateful Dead perform in Copenhagen in 1972. Their band rose to fame promoted by a grassroots network of fans.

By 1967, the group was attracting large crowds drawn to the group's music, which combined folk, jazz, country, electronic noise, long drum solos, and straight-ahead rock and roll.

The Grateful Dead improvised extended jams. These audio roller-coaster rides were designed for listeners who were often high on LSD and other drugs. The group's non-compromising sound prompted the Dead's lyricist Robert Hunter to call his band "a machine-eating psychedelic monster."[20] After the Grateful Dead's lead guitarist Jerry Garcia died in 1995, other bands formed within the Deadhead community. The new wave of 1990s indie jam bands included Phish, Dave Matthews, Umphrey's McGee, and My Morning Jacket.

Psychedelic Meets Heavy Metal

In the 1960s, the eighteen- to thirty-five-minute-long jams by the Grateful Dead inspired other bands to create long, improvised rock songs. Perhaps nothing exemplified this new style better than the 1968 song "In-A-Gadda-Da-Vida" by the Los Angeles, California-based Iron Butterfly. The title "In-A-Gadda-Da-Vida" was supposed to be "In the Garden of Eden," but legend has it that organist and lead singer Doug Engle was so intoxicated that he slurred the words when singing the song. Whatever the case, the song is based on a catchy fuzz tone guitar riff that is repeated throughout the seventeen-minute-long song. The memorable drum solo, punctuated by heavy pounding on the tom-tom drums, was imitated by countless groups in subsequent years.

The song "In-A-Gadda-Da-Vida" was initially released as an edited three-minute single, but the long version, which took up an entire side of a long-playing (LP) vinyl album, attracted millions of listeners and became an instant classic. Senior music editor for the online AllMusic guide, Stephen Thomas Erlewine, explains:

> With its endless, droning minor-key riff and mumbled vocals, 'In-A-Gadda-Da-Vida' is arguably the most notorious song of the acid rock era. . . . [The] group was so stoned when they recorded the track that they

could neither pronounce the title . . . or end the track, so it rambles on for a full 17 minutes, which to some listeners sounds like eternity. But that's the essence of its appeal—it's the epitome of heavy psychedelic excess, encapsulating the most indulgent tendencies of the era.[21]

The song was released on an album, also called *In-A-Gadda-Da-Vida*, which stayed on the album charts for 140 weeks, eventually selling more than 30 million copies. The song is considered significant in rock history because it marks a time when psychedelic music morphed into proto-hard rock and heavy metal by employing guitar distortion, dramatic macho singing, and driving drums.

The Beatles Move to the Garage

In an era when music experimentation was rampant, the heavy garage band sound also caught the attention of one of the most influential groups in pop music history: the Beatles. In November 1968, the Beatles released their ninth album, titled *The Beatles*, but commonly referred to as *The White Album*. The songs on the double album range from the sublime "Dear Prudence" to the silly "Wild Honey Pie" and the avant-garde "Revolution 9." Nearly all of the thirty tracks on *The White Album* pushed the boundaries of rock and roll, but two of these songs also made significant contributions to alternative rock by elevating the garage band sound to a riotous new level.

The song "Everybody's Got Something to Hide Except Me and My Monkey," written by Beatles guitarist John Lennon, begins with a sharp, metallic guitar riff over drummer Ringo Starr's deep, thumping bass drum. Lennon begins singing in a crazed shout as an agitated, clanging cowbell fades in and out, pushing the tempo of the fast-paced song. The ringing musical mix combines Paul McCartney's ascending bass lines and a ticklish lead guitar riff played between the beats by George Harrison.

Lennon's contribution to what would become alt-rock combines various elements of punk, new wave, grunge, and metal within the two-minute, twenty-five-second song.

Bands that recorded "Everybody's Got Something to Hide Except Me and My Monkey" in later years cover the range of alternative music styles. The tune was performed by the grunge group Soundgarden, indie rockers the Feelies, the British hard rock band 60ft Dolls, hard-core punker Kristin Hersh, the punk band the Chameleons, and the indie jam band Phish.

Helter Skelter

Paul McCartney's groundbreaking contribution to heavy metal, grunge, and punk can be heard on "Helter Skelter." When McCartney created the song, he set out to make the loudest, rawest, dirtiest rock song ever written, and he succeeded. At the time "Helter Skelter" was released, there was nothing like it.

As the title implies, "Helter Skelter" is disorderly, confused, and chaotic. The song first came to life in the summer of 1968 as a twenty-seven-minute, drug-fueled jam. When it was recorded in September, it wound up as the

The Beatles' experiments with sounds and music in the late 1960s contributed to the alternative rock sound.

most disruptive four-and-a-half minutes on *The White Album*. McCartney's screaming vocals are enhanced by excessive echo and reverb. The guitars clatter and clang, and the thumping bass guitar is ever-so-slightly out of tune.

Frank Zappa Freaks Out

Guitarist, singer, and rock composer Frank Zappa was noted for his scathingly funny songs about the greed and idiocy rampant in popular culture. In 1995, when Rykodisc reissued fifty Frank Zappa albums on CD, the record label called Zappa one of the great icons of alternative music. Music journalist Chris Smith describes the revolutionary aspects of the first album written by Zappa and played by his group Mothers of Invention:

Zappa burst onto the scene in the summer of 1966 with *Freak Out!*, one of the most mind-bending debuts in the history of rock, as well as one of the first studio double albums. Exhibiting a dazzling combination of jazz, pop, doo-wop, bubble-gum, protest, punk, close-harmony group vocals, spoken word . . . and satire, the album disintegrated rather than stretched the boundaries of what was possible in a rock album. *Freak Out!* demonstrated a mastery of the un-

predictable and unorthodox while somehow maintaining ties to the pop craftsmanship it ridicules. . . . Zappa and the Mothers sought to tell it like it is rather than like it should be, lambasting the hypocrisy of both the status quo and the counterculture, even taking potshots at themselves in the process.

Chris Smith. *101 Albums That Changed Popular Music.* New York: Oxford University Press, 2009, p. 39.

Frank Zappa was one of the great icons of alternative music.

The overall effect is a tooth-rattling song that likely induces headaches in some listeners. American musicologist Alan W. Pollack explains the power of "Helter Skelter": "[Crank] this one up some late night when you're home alone and all the lights are off, and it's guaranteed to raise the hair on the back of your neck; to scare and unsettle you."[22] Like "Everybody's Got Something to Hide," "Helter Skelter" was covered by a stellar list of alternative rock bands.

Proto-Indie Values

Musicians have always been inspired by those who came before them. Musical experimentation was extensive in the second half of the 1960s, and the sounds of the era inspired generations of musicians that followed. Alternative rockers can look back at a time when musical creativity, emotional expression, and social criticism were valued over the commercial demands of the mainstream music marketplace. For alternative rockers, the 1960s provides a rich history of sound and verse from which to mine a steady stream of musical gold.

CHAPTER 2

The Birth of Punk

During the late 1960s, while hippies danced to the sunny music of the Grateful Dead in San Francisco's Golden Gate Park, the streets of New York, New York, were much more somber. A series of urban riots had left some New York City neighborhoods, such as Harlem and the South Bronx, with block after block of burned and abandoned buildings, giving the city the appearance of a war zone. Times Square, in the heart of New York, was a haven for pimps, prostitutes, drug addicts, muggers, and gangsters. Unlike in the wealthy, glittering New York City of the twenty-first century, poverty, crime, and despair were rampant in the 1960s.

Few songwriters cared to address New York's problems during what was generally an optimistic era. However, guitarist and songwriter Lou Reed was attracted to the dark and wild side of New York street life with its unique blend of hustlers, artists, musicians, and poets. By the mid-1960s, Reed was composing songs that addressed taboo subjects such as hopelessness, alienation, violence, sexual deviancy, and drug addiction. Reed's music was nihilistic, meaning the songs described a world in which nothing had meaning, purpose, or value.

Reed's nihilistic attitude was expressed by his band, the Velvet Underground. The group rejected traditionally accepted pop music elements, such as harmony, hooks, and danceable rhythms, while singing about sex, drugs, and ravaged romance. While this was a shocking direction for a 1960s rock band to take, Reed found his inspiration in serious literature, such as the novels of William Faulkner, whose characters were often suicidal alcoholics, addicts, neurotics, and racists. As Reed explained in a 1989 interview: "I never in a million years thought people would be outraged by what I was doing. You could go to your neighborhood bookstore and get [books filled with] any of that."[23]

The nihilistic lyrics and musical attitude of the Velvet Underground would come to dominate punk rock and other forms of alternative music in the following years. This led music professor Scott D. Lipscomb to call the Velvet Underground the "godfathers of punk [who pioneered a] unique style which was decades ahead of its time."[24]

"Abrasive Three-Chord Rockers"

The Velvet Underground came together in 1964, when Reed began playing with British musician John Cale. At the time they began their musical collaboration, Reed was working as an unsuccessful songwriter in New York's Brill Building, where other young composers produced number-one smash pop hits like "Da Do Ron Ron," "What's New, Pussycat?" and "You've Lost That Lovin' Feelin'." Reed's Brill Building songwriting credit was a single silly novelty song about a dance called the Ostrich. Cale, on the other hand, was an extremely serious and dedicated musician. He was a classically trained multi-instrumentalist, proficient on viola, cello, piano, and saxophone. At the time he met Reed, Cale was active in the New York avant-garde noise music scene. To create noise music, composers combine electronic sounds, recorded industrial noise, and the dissonant racket that can be made with hammers, garbage cans, bottles, car parts, and other nontraditional instruments.

One of Reed's most controversial songs, "Heroin," was written in 1964, during an era of peppy Beatles songs and sing-along garage rock. "Heroin" was about using and abusing the highly addictive drug heroin. The song, sung

by Reed in his trademark flat monotone, was widely condemned for glorifying heroin use. Cale was impressed by the song's droning two-chord structure and the tempo, which sped up and slowed down several times. In 1965, Reed and Cale joined with guitarist Sterling Morrison and nineteen-year-old drummer Maureen "Mo" Tucker to form the Velvet Underground.

Although Tucker had never played an instrument before joining the group, her unusual approach would come to be imitated by alt-rock drummers in later decades. Unlike most drummers of the time, Tucker played standing up. Her stripped-down four-piece drum kit consisted only of a snare drum, two tom-toms that have a low tone, and an upturned bass drum that is usually played with a foot pedal. And Tucker played her drums with mallets rather than sticks, which gave the sound a deep, cavernous rumble.

On one occasion, after her drums were stolen, Tucker played a gig pounding on garbage cans she found in an alley behind the bar. Culture critic Michael Sandlin describes Tucker's unique musical approach:

The Velvet Underground—John Cale, Lou Reed, and Mo Tucker (left to right)—though relatively obscure, had a great influence on other musicians.

Her distinct, cymbal-less drumming style propelled the Velvets' abrasive three-chord rockers, and anchored the band's free-form sonic mayhem. Strictly self-taught, Moe . . . inaugurated the very idea of the female-as-instrumentalist into the collective rock n' roll consciousness, and set a lasting precedent.[25]

Anti-Rock and Anti-Melodies

The Velvet Underground's debut album, *The Velvet Underground and Nico*, is filled with Reed's dark, brooding songs. While the record failed to sell in large numbers, it was highly influential, as music journalist Chris Smith explains:

Cale was fascinated with the anti-rock notion of drones, and would create low, moody anti-melodies with his viola to compliment Reed's speak-singing vocals and gritty lyrics about sex, drugs, and [cross-dressing] in New York City's dark underbelly. To call the band uncommercial is an understatement . . . the heady experimentation of the Velvets never had a chance. . . . Musically, the album is surprisingly eclectic, with Cale and Reed combining crunchy rock, rhythm and blues, free jazz, and avant-garde experimentation in a brew that would influence punk . . . new wave, heavy metal, and grunge over the next three decades.[26]

Iggy Pop's "Grimy, Noisy"

John Cale left the Velvet Underground in 1968 due to creative differences with Lou Reed. In 1970, Reed disbanded the group to start a solo career. Although the group's career was relatively short, Brian Eno, an avant-garde rock musician and producer of several acclaimed U2 albums, summed up the band's impact: "Only five thousand people ever bought a Velvet Underground album, but every single one of them started a band."[27] This comment, clearly an exaggeration as the Velvet Underground sold several hundred thousand records, does hold some truth, though, because the group's sound inspired many who heard their music.

One of the musicians who was moved by the music of this

moody New York band was living nearly five hundred miles from Manhattan. James Newell Osterberg, known as Iggy Pop, lived in Detroit, Michigan, which is called the Motor City because it is the corporate home to car manufacturers General Motors, Chrysler, and Ford. With its smoke-belching factories, gritty neighborhoods, and periodic race riots, the Motor City both alienated and inspired Iggy Pop and his band, the Stooges, which formed in 1967.

The raucous sounds of the auto assembly lines motivated Pop to make industrial noise. In early concerts, he held a microphone to a running vacuum cleaner and household blender as guitarist Ron Asheton laid down screaming walls of ear-shattering feedback with his electric guitar and amplifier. The cacophony was enhanced by Ron's brother, drummer Scott Asheton, who pounded wildly on an oil

Iggy Pop of the Stooges rides the crowd during a 1970 concert in Cincinnati, Ohio.

drum with a ball-peen hammer. Dave Alexander wailed away on his bass guitar, which he could barely play, thrumming the strings to produce a low, gut-churning rumble. The resulting roar was said to sound like a jet plane landing in a barroom.

Despite their seeming lack of commercial potential, the Stooges were signed by the prestigious Elektra Records label in 1969. The band's first album, *The Stooges*, was produced by John Cale, who took work as a record producer after he quit the Velvet Underground. The Stooges only had five original songs at the time, and wrote three more the night before the recording session was scheduled, playing them for the first time in the studio. When *The Stooges* was released, it was savaged by critics and ignored by the public. AllMusic editors Stephen Thomas Erlewine and Mark Deming describe the album's sound as "grimy, noisy and relentlessly bleak rock & roll."[28]

"Long, Droning Scars"

By the time of their first album, all of the members of the Stooges were addicted to various drugs, including heroin and amphetamines. Iggy Pop's onstage behavior was becoming more outrageous by the day. At gigs, the band created jarring industrial noise music while Pop smeared his chest with meat and peanut butter, pulled down his pants, and yelled obscenities at the audience. People in the crowd reacted by pelting the band with ice cubes, jelly beans, eggs, and even full beer bottles. Numbed by drugs, Pop picked up pieces of broken beer bottles and dragged the sharp, jagged shards across his arms and chest as the crowd cheered him on. Dripping with blood, sweat, beer, and various foods, Pop would dive off the stage, fall to the floor, and wiggle like a snake between the legs of spectators. According to Dave Marsh: "[The Stooges] didn't advocate revolt; they acted revolting. . . . They proceeded to slash long, droning scars across the musical landscape with chordless, feedback-clouded credos like 'I Wanna Be Your Dog' and 'Search and Destroy.'"[29]

The Stooges' next album, *Funhouse*, was produced by

A Sonic Account of Collapse

In the 1960s, Detroit, Michigan, was home to "the Big Three" automakers—General Motors, Chrysler, and Ford—and led the world in car manufacturing. American cars were large and powerful, but were notorious gas guzzlers. This was not a problem for the Big Three until 1973, when the Organization of Petroleum Exporting Countries (OPEC) raised the price of oil and cut production. This created gas shortages and a steep decline in American auto sales. Dave Marsh, who calls Detroit "Autoworld," describes the economic conditions that inspired the music of Iggy Pop and the Stooges:

> Iggy and the Stooges shaped their sound and sensibility . . . on the fringes of Detroit, just as the postwar prosperity of Autoworld disintegrated. . . . The Motor City's working class went from being the richest in the world to double-digit unemployment with a barely discernable transition. The three albums Iggy and the Stooges made between 1969 and 1973—*The Stooges, Funhouse,* and *Raw Power*—comprise a sonic account of their home territory's all-front (economic, social, political, spiritual) collapse. Since the collapse ultimately took on national and worldwide dimensions, these three albums, for all their crudity, now rank among the most profound and powerful records ever created.

Dave Marsh. *Louie Louie*. New York: Hyperion, 1993, p. 158.

Don Gallucci, keyboardist for the Kingsmen, who played on the classic song "Louie Louie." *Funhouse* is a dark, menacing, messy conglomeration of electronic noise, throbbing beats, and Pop's anguished screams. Although the album was trashed by critics and initially sold less than ten thousand copies, it is now credited as influencing a new breed of punks, noise rockers, and grunge musicians. As Marsh explains: "In

1969 they received the most gruesome reviews of any band in the history of rock criticism; by 1975, they were the darlings of the music press."[30] The Stooges only released one more album, *Raw Power*, which was largely ignored when released in 1973. The band disintegrated soon after.

CBGB & OMFUG

Despite their short careers, the Stooges and other proto-punks laid the foundation for the punk rock movement. As music professor Larry Starr and professor of arts and culture Christopher Waterman write: "The amateur energy of [1960s] garage band rock 'n' roll, the artsy nihilism of the Velvet Underground, and raw energy and abandon of the Stooges . . . converged in the mid-1970s in New York City's burgeoning club scene."[31]

The center for this explosive energy was a New York nightclub called CBGB & OMFUG, opened by Hilly Kristal in 1973. Kristal originally hoped to feature bands that played acoustic country and blues music. The letters in the club's name CBGB & OMFUG stood for "Country, Bluegrass, Blues & Other Music for Urban Gormandizers." A gormandizer is a glutton, in this case a person who voraciously consumes music.

CBGB was located on Bowery Street, which gave its name to the impoverished neighborhood also known as Skid Row. The area was a magnet for homeless alcoholics called Bowery bums. Poet and punk rock singer-songwriter Patti Smith recalls the scene: "It was the street of winos and they would often have fires going in large cylindrical trash cans to keep warm, to cook, or light their cigarettes."[32]

Around the time CBGB opened, New York was experiencing the worst economic crisis in a generation. Rising gas prices, economic inflation, and widespread factory layoffs sparked a national recession responsible for pushing New York City to the brink of bankruptcy. The mid-1970s was a low point for the city, a time when garbage piled up, parks and libraries closed, empty storefronts dominated the cityscape, and a soaring crime and social unrest created hopelessness among residents.

Crude Music

New York's despair provided artistic inspiration to the nihilistic poets, painters, and musicians who were renting cheap Bowery lofts for around $100 a month near CBGB. Among this group were two young musicians from Lexington, Kentucky, Richard Meyers and Tom Miller, who reinvented themselves as bassist Richard Hell and lead guitarist Tom Verlaine. They formed the band Television with the addition of lead guitarist Jimmy Ripp and drummer Billy Ficca. The group's first gig, at CBGB in 1974, was unpaid, on a Sunday when the bar was usually closed.

Television wrote songs with obscene, unprintable titles or those with jokey names like "If I Hadn't Lost My Head, I Wouldn't Have Lost My Hat." The group's music was called street rock before the term *punk* was coined. The sound was informed by garage rock and proto-punk. As Hell explains, Television's music was "a return to the values of the Kingsmen, and the Sonics and Them and The Velvet Underground . . . ecstatic, explosive guitar . . . [but] more driving and crazed."[33] Hilly Kristal offers his own opinion on

The band Television perform at iconic New York club CBGB in 1977. Their music was called street rock before the term punk *was coined.*

Television's sound: "I thought it was crude music . . . it was hard to take. It was very loud and abrasive. It was not what I liked in music . . . because they were not musicians."[34]

Kristal did like one thing about Television: The ragtag group of amateurs attracted a dedicated, hard-drinking audience. During subsequent gigs, CBGB was packed when the group played. Television also brought in a parade of punk musicians who would go on to permanently change the sound of rock and roll. For example, singer Debbie Harry and her boyfriend, guitarist Chris Stein, were early Television fans. In 1974, Harry and Stein formed the group Blondie, which opened for Television at CBGB. By 1977, Blondie was one of the biggest pop groups in the world.

"Drunk and Disorderly"

The poet Patti Smith was among the neighborhood hipsters attracted to Television's crazed performances. Smith wrote verses inspired by Bob Dylan, by the nineteenth-century French poet Arthur Rimbaud, and by 1950s Beat poets like Allen Ginsberg and William Burroughs. Intrigued by the poetic verses of Television songs, Smith decided to create her own punk rock. She recruited guitarist Lenny Kaye to provide an improvised musical sound track while she made up poetry on the spot. Kaye commented on the musical collaboration: "There was no one else doing anything remotely like us at that time . . . the improvisation, the freedom, the openness to the moment."[35]

Smith and Kaye formed the Patti Smith Group in early 1975, adding a drummer, bassist, and pianist. On Valentine's Day 1975, the Patti Smith Group played its first gig at CBGB. A month later, Smith began a five-week running engagement as Television's opening act. She later recalled the scene: "It was the greatest atmosphere to perform in. It was conspiratorial. It was physical, and that's what rock 'n' roll's all about—sexual tension and being drunk and disorderly."[36]

Smith was the high priestess of punk who entranced the audience nightly. Rock critic Charles Shaar Murray described her performance at CBGB: "She stands there machine-gunning out her lines, singing a bit and talking a bit, in total control, riding it and steering it with a twist of a shoulder here, a flick of the wrist there—scaled down, bird-like movements that carry an almost unbelievable degree of power."[37]

Smith was the first of the CBGB alumni to receive a recording contract from a major label. Along with her stunning originals, Smith covered two classic garage rock songs on her debut album, *Horses*. The record is described by musicologist Peter Doggett:

> The album opened with Patti declaring "Jesus died for somebody's sins but not mine," and ended with an "Elegie" for Jimi Hendrix. The 40-minute journey between those two points incorporated classic rock motifs ("Gloria," "Land of 10,000 Dances"), tightly structured original material that matched those anthems for impact, and two lengthy flurries of free verse on which Smith sounded possessed by angels and devils in equal measure.[38]

Smith opened her follow-up album, *Radio Ethiopia*, with ten minutes of poetry recited over relentless screeching

Patti Smith, a poet and punk rocker, was known as the "priestess of punk."

feedback and other noise. Although the primitive sound was panned by the press, Smith remained an innovative and influential force well into the twenty-first century.

The Ill-Mannered Ramones

Patti Smith's music might have been angry and loud, but her lyrical wanderings were built on strong, intellectual foundations. In contrast, the second CBGB band signed by a major label, the Ramones, had no such cerebral basis. The group's lack of intellectual underpinnings are revealed in their song titles: "Suzy is a Headbanger," "Gimme Gimme Shock Treatment," and "Now I Wanna Sniff Some Glue."

The Ramones was a group of unrelated musicians who all used the surname Ramone—Joey Ramone, Dee Dee Ramone, Marky Ramone, and Tommy Ramone. Dee Dee, a self-described manic depressive, called his bandmates "a bunch of ill-mannered lowlifes."[39] The Ramones dressed like 1950s bikers in ripped jeans and black leather jackets. Each band member wore a hairstyle called a pudding bowl, which was long in the front and short on the sides and back. After the Ramones' CBGB debut, Hilly Kristal commented, "The Ramones were even worse than Television. Their equipment kept breaking down and they were constantly yelling at each other. They only had a few songs but they would never get all the way through any of them."[40]

Despite Kristal's criticism, the Ramones quickly became the stars of the burgeoning CBGB punk scene, eventually playing the club more than a hundred times. Those who attended Ramones shows heard songs that were very loud, excessively fast, and extremely short—characteristics that defined the punk sound in the late 1970s. Music writer Matt Diehl describes the songs of the Ramones as informed by an "ironic, taboo-threatening humor. . . . [A] primal three-chord monte, reducing rock and roll to its barest, fastest essential. Its monochrome guitars, village-idiot yelling, and sheer velocity set the tone—song titles like 'Blitzkrieg Bop' and 'Chainsaw' served as truth in advertising manifestos, perfectly capturing the band's sound in words."[41]

In 1976, the group released its eponymous, or self-named, debut album *Ramones*, which had four songs and clocked in at twenty-nine minutes, four seconds. The band spent only about $6,400 and took seven days to make the record. By comparison, one of the most popular albums of the era, *Hotel California*, by the country rock band the Eagles, was recorded over the course of eight months for $500,000. Most of the nine songs on the forty-three-minute *Hotel California* are epics lasting five to seven minutes.

In the spirit of the Velvet Underground, the short songs on *Ramones* cover shocking topics ranging from Nazism to drug abuse and male prostitution. *Creem* editor and *Rolling Stone* contributor Ben Edmunds describes *Ramones*:

> [The album] showcased the band's distillation of influences from bubblegum pop to horror movies to real life. Lead track "Blitzkrieg Bop" opened with the band's "Hey! Ho! Let's Go!" rallying cry. "Beat on the Brat" saw Joey recalling the boredom and "rich ladies with bratty kids" of [suburban New York]. Joey's lyrics on "Judy is a Punk" regaled us with a true-life tale of two Ramones fans, Jackie and Judy. "53rd & 3rd" depicts a pick-up spot for male prostitutes who'd turn tricks to buy heroin, a subject songwriter Dee Dee refused to discuss, fueling speculation that it was autobiographical.[42]

The rock press loved the album *Ramones*. Critics described the record variously as loud, fast, stupid, happy, and simple. Record buyers mostly ignored the album, although it briefly landed at number 111 on the *Billboard* Top 200 album chart. Although Americans were not yet ready for the fast, furious sound of the Ramones, the band was loved by British audiences who viewed them as the saviors of rock and roll.

Anarchy in the U.K.

When the Ramones played their first English gig at London's Roundhouse, they ignited a punk rock rebellion in the United Kingdom. Dozens of musicians were in attendance, and some would go on to form their own punk bands, including Johnny Rotten and Sid Vicious of the Sex Pistols and Mick Jones and Paul Simonon of the Clash.

The Sex Pistols was the first British band to grab hold of the new sound. The story of the group's rocket rise to fame and rapid self-destruction has become the stuff of punk rock legend. The Sex Pistols was formed in 1976, not by musicians but by Malcolm McLaren, a shopkeeper. McLaren owned a clothing store called SEX that sold punk rock fashions and bizarre clothes made of leather and rubber.

McLaren was inspired to recruit musicians for a band after visiting New York City in 1972 and meeting the proto-punk band New York Dolls. The all-male Dolls dressed as women, complete with makeup and high heels, something considered outrageous in the early 1970s. The rocking sounds of the Dolls inspired the Ramones and other punkers in later years.

After attending some early CBGB shows, McLaren decided to import punk music and fashion to England. He approached Television's Richard Hell with the idea of starting a punk band in London. Hell is credited with inventing punk rock fashions—he was among the first to wear spiked hair, ripped jeans, and torn T-shirts held together with safety pins. Hell turned down the offer, but according to McLaren: "Richard Hell was a definite 100% inspiration [for the Sex Pistols]. . . . I was going to imitate it and transform it into something more English."[43]

Sid Vicious and lead singer Johnny Rotten of the Sex Pistols during their first US concert in 1978.

"Glammed-out Punkers"

The New York Dolls invented a new genre called glam or glitter rock and in doing so became one of the most outrageous groups in the early punk scene. The group was formed in 1971 in New York City, and their musical influences included a wide range of styles from 1950s rockers to the Rolling Stones and the Stooges. In a review of the group's first album, *New York Dolls*, *Rolling Stone* referred to the group as "Glammed-out punkers [who] drip with sleaze and style."

The sound of the New York Dolls was raunchy, sloppy, shrill, and crude. It was garage rock overlaid with lead singer David Johansen's off-key singing. Critics slammed the Dolls' sound, but it was the band's appearance that received the most attention. Members of the all-male band wore women's wigs, fishnet stockings, tutus, bright red lipstick, eye shadow, ostrich feathers, and high-heeled boots.

The New York Dolls' outrageous cross-dressing look was the start of the glam or glitter rock movement.

This helped the Dolls attract a small, devoted following in New York. The group only released two albums, *New York Dolls* (1973) and *Too Much Too Soon* (1974), but their influence was enormous. The group provided a blueprint for the glam rock style promoted by superstar David Bowie in the early 1970s and later imitated by arena-filling rock bands like KISS and Alice Cooper.

Quoted in Joe Levy, ed. *The 500 Greatest Albums of All Time*. New York: Wenner Books, 2005, p. 163.

McLaren recruited three amateur musicians who hung around his shop, guitarist Steve Jones, bassist Glen Matlock, and drummer Paul Cook. They could barely play their instruments, but they were better than John Lydon, who was hired as the band's lead singer. Lydon was an angry, alienated teen with acne scars who died his hair green and wore a homemade T-shirt bearing the message, "I Hate Pink Floyd." His audition consisted of shrieking Alice Cooper's "Eighteen" into a fake microphone made from a shower-head as the song played on the store jukebox.

Lydon was hired on the spot and given the punk nickname Johnny Rotten due to his poor dental hygiene. McLaren explains how he came up with the name Sex Pistols: "Taking their name partly from the shop, SEX, I then added the word Pistols. I was looking for . . . a name that could act as a metaphor. Here was a band, the Sex Pistols, that would—and *did*—shoot down anything we didn't like, which in our case was absolutely everything."[44]

Although Rotten's voice was terrible, he had a notebook full of poetry. As the Sex Pistols played loud, abrasive, gritty punk rock, Rotten stabbed out verses he had written about abortion, anarchy, apathy, fascism, and violence. The group's shocking music and sometimes violent stage behavior helped the group build a steady following among London's disaffected youth. At the time, London, much like New York City, was wracked with economic problems. Workers throughout the country were on strike, huge piles of garbage filled London streets, and extreme nihilism was in fashion among the young.

After less than a year of playing together, the Sex Pistols were signed by EMI, one of the world's biggest record companies. In the group's first single, "Anarchy in the U.K.," Rotten declares himself an Antichrist and an anarchist in an atonal, sneering yowl. "Anarchy in the U.K." was a call to arms for England's frustrated and alienated youth, according to singer-songwriter Brody Dalle: "The Sex Pistols came around like a political movement. There was political unrest and depression in England. No money, no jobs . . . just a grey, drab life."[45]

"Anarchy in the U.K." dropped like a bomb, and negative publicity surrounding the Sex Pistols caused EMI to fire the band. The group was signed by another label, but its next song, 1977's "God Save the Queen," was even more explosive. The lyrics mock Britain's Queen Elizabeth, saying that she is not a human being, she is part of a fascist regime, and there is no future in England. Millions of citizens in the

Mainstream Music in the 1970s

In the mid-1970s, the FM radio airwaves were dominated by highly marketable pop music by the likes of Elton John, Bachman-Turner Overdrive, the Average White Band, and the Eagles. Punk rockers like Patti Smith, the Ramones, and the Sex Pistols rebelled against this mainstream music scene, described by Dutch punk rock musician and journalist Henrik Bech Poulsen:

> The rock music climate in the mid-70s had stagnated into a safe, boring, bland, complacent, dull and pathetic malady. Any elements of excitement, danger or passion were long gone. Many of the rock and roll musicians in the major bands had become self-indulgent bloated millionaires, removed several galaxies from their fans. The music was over-arranged, over-produced and often featured extended guitar solos and progressive or symphonic elements. Punk rock showed the world that it is not the size of the weapons that matters, but the ferocity of the attack.
>
> On the rock music barometer of success and popularity, stadium bands (such as Queen, Pink Floyd and Fleetwood Mac) reigned supreme prior to 1977. If you weren't an arena mega-group, you could basically forget about being in a rock band.

Henrik Bech Poulsen. *'77: The Year of Punk & New Wave*. London: Helter Skelter Publishing, 2005, p. 13.

United Kingdom considered insults to the queen to be treasonous and were outraged by "God Save the Queen." The record was banned from British radio stations, but still sold more than 150,000 copies in ten days after its release.

The Pistols released their first album, *Never Mind the Bollocks, Here's the Sex Pistols*, in November 1977, and it rocketed to number one on the British album charts. By this time, the Sex Pistols were an international music sensation. Matlock, who was one of the group's better musicians, had been replaced on bass by Sid Vicious, who could not play at all. (Bass parts on Sex Pistols records were played by Jones.)

Vicious often played Sex Pistols shows drunk and drugged out of his mind on speed and heroin. Unable to play bass, he acted more like a performance artist, playing the part of the quintessential punk rock maniac in the mold of Iggy Pop. Vicious swaggered around the stage, banging people over the head with his heavy guitar, spitting on the audience, cutting himself, screaming obscenities, and swilling bourbon out of the bottle.

"The Infrastructure to an Alternative Society"

After the Sex Pistols played San Francisco, California, in 1978, the American West Coast punk movement, led by bands like Black Flag and the Dead Kennedys, took off. However, as a band based on anger, nihilism, and self-destruction, the Sex Pistols could not last long and ultimately broke up at the end of 1978. A little more than a year later, Sid Vicious was dead, killed by a heroin overdose.

Despite the group's short career, the Sex Pistols also helped launch a worldwide punk movement still active today. Dozens of British Sex Pistols fans went on to form their own groups, including the Clash, Siouxsie and the Banshees, and the Police. Malcolm McLaren comments on the lasting influence of the band he put together: "From one tiny shop . . . we had created our own code of living, our own laws, our own identity. In other words we had created the infrastructure to an alternative society."[46]

CHAPTER 3

Indie Is a Way of Life

In the early 1980s, the blistering, high-speed sound of punk rock was transforming into something new. A new wave of musicians, inspired by punk's stripped-down music and rebellious attitude, was adding creative new elements to the basic sound. These acts melded punk rock with musical styles as diverse as 1950s rockabilly, 1960s funk, and Jamaican ska, an early form of reggae. Emerging sounds such as beat-heavy hip hop, electronic dance, disco, and African pop were also being incorporated into the new music of the 1980s.

In the early part of the decade, bands that melded punk with various other musical styles were called post-punk or new wave. New-wave artists were largely independent musicians who survived using do-it-yourself (DIY) methods. Unlike the rock supergroups of the era, which traveled in private jets and recorded for multinational record companies, new wavers recorded for small record labels, toured in beat-up vehicles, played small venues, and expanded their fan base through fanzines and word-of-mouth marketing. The reality of this life is described by music journalist Richard Cromelin as, "endless drives in the van, bad food . . . shoestring recording sessions, hellhole nightclubs, [and] sleeping on floors."[47]

The Clash

The Clash was no stranger to the hardships experienced by musical misfits. Formed in London in 1976, the Clash was part of the new wave of punk bands inspired by the Sex Pistols. The group, formed by singer-guitarist Joe Strummer and lead guitarist Mick Jones, was signed to a major label and had several hit singles on Britain's Top 40 charts in the late 1970s.

Although the public perceived Strummer and Jones to be major rock stars, both lived with Jones' grandmother in an apartment in a public housing complex. They could not afford their own apartments because the Clash was in debt to its record company, CBS, for recording and touring expenses. The money was deducted from record sales and the band members received almost nothing.

The Clash was part of a new wave of punk bands inspired by the Sex Pistols.

Before making the album *London Calling* in 1979, Strummer and Jones, along with Clash bassist Paul Simonon and drummer Nicky "Topper" Headon, could barely afford

to buy clothes. According to Simonon, the Clash rehearsed in a garage "with one light and filthy carpeting on the walls for soundproofing. We felt that we were struggling, about to slide down a slope or something, grasping with our fingernails. And there was nobody there to help us."[48]

Despite the group's precarious financial situation, the Clash was at its creative peak in late 1979. When *London Calling* was released in the United States in 1980, it was hailed by critics as a major step forward for punk rock because of its innovative melding of musical styles. On "Brand New Cadillac," Strummer sings in the quivery, quaking style of 1950s rockabilly star Gene Vincent, as Jones plays twangy lead guitar riffs straight out of a 1960s surf song. On "Rudie Can't Fail" and "Wrong 'Em Boyo," the Clash

Ska's "Upside-Down R&B"

During the 1950s and 1960s, waves of Jamaican immigrants moved to the United Kingdom to work in factories. They brought from home the sounds of ska and introduced them to white musicians. The style has since been incorporated into various forms of alternative rock in the U.K. and the United States. The Jamaican sound is described by British music journalist Simon Reynolds:

> Ska began at the end of the fifties as a Jamaican twist on black American dance music from New Orleans, "upside-down R&B," as guitarist Ernest Ranglin put it. The term "ska" is most likely derived from the characteristic ska-ska-ska-ska attack of the rhythm guitar stressing the "afterbeat" [or backbeat], which intensifies the music's choppy, chugging feel. The [Clash] took the staccato pulse of sixties ska and amped it up with punk's frenetic energy. . . . The sixties source invariably sounds sluggish in comparison, less aggressive.

Simon Reynolds. *Rip It Up and Start Again*. New York: Penguin Books, 2005, p. 231.

fuses the danceable backbeats of Jamaican ska music with punk's frantic force. The group even dabbled in disco, incorporating an insistent disco syncopated drumbeat into the arrangement of "Lost in the Supermarket."

By combining the wide array of musical styles into a new sound, the Clash provided the first early links between punk and alternative rock. This prompted *Rolling Stone* to list *London Calling* at number eight among the 500 Greatest Albums Of All Time, between classic records by Bob Dylan, the Beatles, and the Rolling Stones.

In August 1980, the Clash began recording their next album, *Sandinista!* The record was a triple album—six sides of vinyl filled with thirty-six songs that spanned 144 minutes of punk, rap, funk, rock and roll, R&B, soul, jazz, gospel, electronic noise, ska, and reggae. The album is recognized today as one of the groundbreaking records of the post-punk era.

Despite the group's innovative music and critical success, the Clash continually battled CBS. Company executives believed the band's radical political lyrics were too controversial for the American public. Like most other bands on a major record label, the Clash had few rights when it came to creative control over its songs, image, and artwork. While group members tried to convince CBS that their music was acceptable to their fans, record executives had final veto power over album content. Although the Clash finally prevailed, their negative experiences, along with financial difficulties, caused them to break up not long after *Sandinista!* was released.

Taking a Chance with Indie Labels

In an effort to fight back against unjust music industry practices, a new generation of musicians and music entrepreneurs founded independent, or indie, record labels in the early 1980s. The indie labels gave artists much more control over writing, recording, promoting, and distributing their music—and gave them a bigger share of the profits. This was not a perfect system. As music journalist Kaya Oakes writes, making the decision to go with an indie label carried its own risks for a band: "The odds of making money were theoretically not as good on an indie label since their distribution was more limited and most radio stations ignored indie releases; however, given the fact that so many bands got screwed by majors, they were often willing to sacrifice the chance to get rich for the chance to do what they wanted."[49]

Black Flag Is Damaged

In California, a new style of music was emerging that synthesized heavy metal and punk rock into what music professor Steve Waksman calls "the metal/punk continuum."[50] The continuum produced hard-core punk, thrash metal, and more extreme offshoots such as grindcore, industrial metal,

Henry Rollins, left, and Greg Ginn of Black Flag perform in 1982. They are credited with creating the hardcore punk sound.

The Benefits of Indie Labels

Indie music journalist Kaya Oakes explains why so many early alternative rock bands signed with indie record labels:

Prior to . . . the 1980s, most bands were still reliant on the major label system for recording, distributing, and promoting their music. . . . Major labels have a history of signing bands to contracts that look like guaranteed moneymaking deals but that often wind up with the band actually in debt to the label when the labels pay enormous advances that the band struggles to make back. The label also controls the band's image and artwork, has the ability to censor its lyrics, and retains legal rights to its music even if the band somehow manages to extricate itself from its contract. When punk bands in the eighties decided to start forming their own record labels in answer to this inherently exploitative scenario, their main motivation was control. If you were signed to an independent label, you had control over how you sounded in the studio, how your album art came out, what the label could and couldn't do to promote and market your music, where you would play shows, and what lyrics you could sing.

Kaya Oakes. *Slanted and Enchanted.* New York: Henry Holt, 2009, p. 45.

and death metal. All these genres shared similar elements, including very short songs featuring heavily distorted guitars, high-speed tempos, explosive drumbeats, and vocals delivered in a shriek or maniacal growl.

The band Black Flag is credited with inventing the hardcore sound. The group is also one of the first to have created its own independent record label, called SST. The label and the band were founded by Black Flag lead guitarist Greg Ginn in 1976 in Hermosa Beach, a community located on the Pacific Ocean in Southern California. Ginn named the band after the popular Black Flag household insecticide. He also liked the name because it paid homage to his favorite band, the heavy metal group Black Sabbath. In addition, a black flag is a symbol of anarchy, a belief system that thrives on rebellion, antiauthoritarianism, anticapitalism, and a general rejection of mainstream beliefs.

Black Flag's sound was one of barely controlled chaos. The group's first full-length studio album, *Damaged*, released in 1981, is a stunning example of the new hard-core sound. *Damaged* features Ginn's piercing, atonal guitar along with Henry Rollins screaming out the lead vocals with agony and anger. Dez Cadena adds a thick, distorted rhythm guitar sound, while bassist Charles Dukowski and drummer Robo push the tempo to breakneck speed. Black Flag's sound, according to Brendan Mullen of the zine *Neutron Bomb*, "fused an aggressive, revved-up take on punk with unapologetic out-and-out heavy-metal riffs pulled from the Unholy Book of Sabbath and [British hard-rock trio] Motorhead."[51]

Rollins had a history of mental depression and violent behavior, and his lyrics on the album are confrontational, antiestablishment, and political. He screams out verses about depression, mental pain, and issues such as the police harassment of local hard-core fans. With the songs on *Damaged*, Rollins was writing about the life he knew.

In the early 1980s, the hard-core scene was as isolated and alienated as its most dedicated fans. Few Los Angeles clubs would book hard-core bands because of their music and their followers. Fans of Black Flag, the Germs, Suicidal Tendencies, and the Minutemen invented a style of dancing called moshing in which they bounced, pounded, and careened into one another. Sometimes this exuberance led to violence. At various gigs, fans destroyed bars. They threw bottles, got into fights, and broke tables, chairs, and windows.

In 1980, the *Los Angeles Times* ran an article about Black Flag under the headline "Violence Sneaks Into the Punk Scene,"[52] which attracted the attention of authorities. Police in Los Angeles and in conservative Southern California beach towns began referring to hard-core music fans as gang members, anarchists, and even terrorists. Hard-core punks were harassed wherever they gathered.

The Zen of Punk and Pop

Black Flag found it easier to play outside Southern California, and during the 1980s, the band toured relentlessly. This helped spread the hard-core sound to regional indie scenes around the country where the music was being reshaped by local musicians. In a profitable feedback loop for Greg Ginn, his label SST signed several bands that were influenced by Black Flag. This was true in Minneapolis, Minnesota, where SST recording artists Hüsker Dü, along with the Replacements and Soul Asylum, diversified the hard-core sound and kicked off one of the fastest-growing indie music scenes in the country.

Hüsker Dü consisted of guitarist Bob Mould, bassist Greg Norton, and drummer Grant Hart. In the early 1980s, the trio sounded like a quintessential hard-core outfit. Hüsker Dü's debut album, *Land Speed Record*, contained seventeen songs and lasted only twenty-six minutes. Mould and Hart were the group's primary songwriters, and in the following years, Hüsker Dü augmented its hard-core sound with other styles of music. According to Hart, "I was challenging the punk stuff with more pop things, and Bob was more into hardcore."[53] The result was the 1984 double album *Zen Arcade*, which exemplifies the punk-pop sonic hybrid. Stephen Thomas Erlewine describes the album:

In many ways, it's impossible to overestimate the impact of . . . *Zen Arcade* on the American rock underground in the '80s. It's the record that exploded the limits of hardcore and what it could achieve. . . . First and foremost, it's a sprawling concept album, even if the concept isn't immediately clear or comprehensible. More important are the individual songs. Both Bob Mould and Grant Hart abandoned the strict "fast, hard, loud" rules of hardcore punk. . . . Without turning down the volume, Hüsker Dü try everything—pop songs, tape experiments, acoustic songs, pianos, noisy psychedelia. . . . It's music that is informed by hardcore punk and indie rock ideals without being limited by them.[54]

After signing with a major label, Warner Bros., and releasing several more albums, Hüsker Dü disbanded in 1987. Although the trio had a cultlike devotion among fans and was beloved by music critics, it never achieved mainstream success. The group's sound was extremely influential,

The Zine Scene

In the early 1980s, the vast majority of Americans did not own personal computers, printers, or copy machines, and the Internet was unknown outside academic circles. During this era, fans of alternative rock created zines about their favorite groups using old-fashioned typewriters. Some zines were handwritten and illustrated. The black-and-white pages were reproduced at copy shops and stapled together by hand. The crude finished products were sold at local record shops and bookstores. Some zine writers had greater ambitions and created higher-quality products. The most popular zines, *Maximum Rock 'n' Roll*, *Flipside*, and *Factsheet 5*, were nationally distributed and attracted an international audience.

Before technology allowed fans to form online music communities, zines were the main source of coverage for local indie bands, record labels, and bar scenes. Zine topics also included politics, fictional stories, and personal accounts of life at school or work. The popularity of zines created an indie literary culture based on the indie music scene.

though, according to Erlewine: "From the Replacements to Nirvana, the Pixies to Superchunk, nearly every major and minor band that appeared in the alternative underground in the late '80s and '90s owed a major debt to Hüsker Dü, whether they were aware of it or not."[55]

MTV's Moral Shame

The rise and fall of Hüsker Dü took place during an era when mainstream entertainment industry forces were forever changing the look and sound of popular music. The music television channel MTV first went on the air in 1981, and by 1983 the station was a worldwide cultural phenomenon. At the time, MTV played videos twenty-four hours a day, seven days a week, and was responsible for making stars of previously unknown British bands like Duran Duran and the Thompson Twins, while pushing the careers of Michael Jackson, Madonna, and Tina Turner into the stratosphere.

Few large-scale musical outlets could have been more abhorrent to lovers of underground, indie culture. MTV videos devalued music while favoring the look and dance moves of the musicians. While hard-core bands were engaged in aggressive anarchy against commercialism, MTV turned music into a commodity to be bought and sold with little question to its worth. In a 1987 article, Greil Marcus clearly states the common indie attitude about MTV: "[Rarely] has an art form been born dead—as is the case of rock video, and its major outlet MTV. . . . MTV is so ugly, so directly productive of [artistic] and moral shame, as to be fundamentally obscene."[56]

Part of the criticism against MTV was that the station promoted an artistic, sanitized version of new-wave music produced by visually attractive British acts like Adam Ant, Tears for Fears, Duran Duran, and Culture Club. These British indie groups took the alienation, aggression, and nihilism of punk rock and decorated it with catchy beats, melodic choruses, and quirky synthesizer licks. Rock journalist Dave Rimmer criticizes this development, writing that British new-wave music was made by "a generation that had come of age during punk, absorbed its methods, learnt its lessons, but ditched its ideals."[57]

While punk rockers might have rejected the artistic pretensions of British new wave, the sound came to dominate MTV virtually overnight. The music was much more appealing to white, suburban rock fans. As Canadian record executive Brad Weir states, new-wave sounds, "while still innovative, were largely de-politicized and could be effectively packaged and sold."[58]

Once in a Lifetime

Not all new-wave music was arty, mindless product for record companies. Members of the American new-wave quartet the Talking Heads rejected the art rock label, even

though three of them attended art school at the Rhode Island School of Design (RISD). The band's lead singer, guitarist, and chief songwriter David Byrne said the term *art rock* implied that "[we didn't] have sincere feelings about our music or we're just flirting with rock and roll and we're too reserved and detached to rock out on stage."[59]

There is little doubt that the Talking Heads were much more reserved when they shared the CBGB stage with the Ramones and Television in 1977. While the Ramones looked like overgrown, out-of-control teenagers, Byrne dressed in a suit and tie. Unlike the distortion-heavy punk rock of the Sex Pistols, the Talking Heads produced a clean, thin sound that defied classification. Byrne's choppy rhythm guitar and Jerry Harrison's textured keyboards produced an exceptionally danceable groove when combined with the distinctive funk beats of bassist Tina Weymouth and drummer Chris Frantz. On songs like 1979's "Life During Wartime," Byrne's peculiar, twitchy vocals blended with the band's edgy rhythm to give the music an agitated, slightly scary feel that would later be emulated by countless alt-rock groups.

The Talking Heads—Jerry Harrison, Tina Weymouth, Chris Frantz, and David Byrne (left to right)—were part of the American new wave.

Byrne's quirky persona translated well to video and made the Talking Heads fixtures on MTV during the channel's early years. One of the most popular Talking Heads videos of the era was for the 1981 song "Once in a Lifetime," about a middle-age man who questions every aspect of his life, including his large automobile and his beautiful home and beautiful wife.

The artistic music video for "Once in a Lifetime," which has been exhibited at the Metropolitan Museum of Art in New York, features multiple images of a nerdy-looking Byrne in a bow tie, suit, and glasses. He jerks his body and limbs as if he is a marionette on strings. Byrne commented on the success of this video in the early days of MTV: "You could do a vaguely experimental film thing as cheaply as you possibly could, and if it was connected to a song, MTV would play it because they needed stuff desperately in those days."[60]

New-Wave Reggae Rock

The British new-wave band the Police also took advantage of MTV's willingness to play cheaply made videos. The Police were formed in 1977 at the height of the punk rock movement by Sting (lead vocals, bass), Andy Summers (guitar), and Stewart Copeland (drums). The trio's music is an upbeat mixture of reggae beats, pop lyrics, and melodies. Their spiky, bleached blond hair, along with Sting's movie star good looks, created an image perfect for MTV.

The Police's breakthrough single, "Roxanne," appeared in 1979 at a time when Top 40 radio was dominated by the disco music of Donna Summer, the Bee Gees, and Gloria Gaynor. The disco sound, which mixes soul, funk, and Latin beats, features a prominent bass line and robotic syncopated beat usually created by a drum machine. While the sound dominated the airwaves, there was a severe backlash against the music by white rock fans. As a result, disco's popularity crashed quickly in 1980, leaving millions of unsold disco albums in warehouses. The death of disco also created problems for radio programmers. Record executive Harold Childs told the Los Angeles Times, "Radio is desperate for rock product. . . . It's scarce out there. The top 40 stations are

being deluged by disco. They're all looking for some white rock-n-roll."[61]

The Police's radio-friendly white, new-wave reggae rock filled the void. By 1983, when the Police released their fourth album, *Synchronicity*, the group was the most commercially successful new-wave band in history. The Police dominated MTV, with several videos from the album in constant rotation. The video of the hit song "Every Breath You Take" ran for fourteen months.

Sting, and his band The Police, were a perfect fit for MTV.

Thrash Metal Headbangers

Although new wave was an outgrowth of punk rock, the sound had a broad appeal. Albums by the Police and the Talking Heads were purchased by the young and old, men and women. Another genre related to punk rock—thrash metal—had a narrower audience of mainly young white teenage males and became very popular in the mid-1980s.

In 1986, MTV began running *Headbangers Ball*, a one-hour show dedicated to heavy metal music. The program, which ran late at night, created a new demand for heavy metal music. *Headbangers Ball* was so popular by 1988 that the show was increased to three hours. The program showed videos by Motorhead, Megadeath, Slayer, and Anthrax. These groups played a new style of heavy metal, referred to as speed metal or thrash metal. The sound combined punk rock's speed, anger, and distortion with musical virtuosity previously associated with groups like Led Zeppelin and Van Halen.

The birth of thrash metal can be traced back to the United Kingdom in the mid-1970s, when Led Zeppelin was the best-selling heavy metal band in the world. At the time, many British metal and punk fans were looking for a new sound that incorporated their angry political and antisocial attitudes. They found it in Motorhead, a power trio founded in 1975 by bassist, singer, and songwriter Ian "Lemmy" Kilmister and originally featuring "Fast" Eddie Clarke on guitar and Phil "Philthy Animal" Taylor on drums.

Rabid, Insatiable Creatures

Motorhead's 1979 album *Overkill*, released by the indie Bronze label, is considered by critics to be among the first records in the metal/punk continuum. *Overkill*'s title track is a two-chord study in thrash metal. It raises the listener's blood pressure with an unrelenting, fast-paced rhythmic momentum that is barely contained. The lyrics describe the physical impact of the music. Lemmy Kilmister screams that the beat goes straight to the spine and the listener must be dead if the song leaves him in his seat.

Thrash fans helped push *Overkill* up to number twenty-four on the British album charts, but Motorhead did not get much respect. Unlike new-wave music, thrash metal was disparaged by critics as a tired sound that should be called old wave. Heavy metal fans ignored the music press. And since they could not hear their music on the radio, they flocked to concerts to support their favorite bands. As critic Paul Rambali wrote in 1983, the thrash metal fan "is the most rabid, devoted, insatiable creature there is, willing to join tens of thousands of his fellow worshippers at the flash bomb altar."[62]

Motorhead, seen here in London in 1978, was the first thrash metal group.

As with other musical styles, there were those who were willing to take an extreme sound and make it even more intense. In this way, thrash metal spawned the death metal sound in the late 1980s. Death metal devotees gave their bands morbid names such Napalm Death, Carcass, Dismember, and Malevolent Creation. These groups played extremely slow, lumbering, distorted heavy metal. Singers sang persistently about death, gore, suffering, torture, and pain in growling or shrieking voices that sounded like monsters from horror films.

The Jangle and Mystery of R.E.M.

While most death metal bands attracted only small cult-like followings, indie rock blew up in a big way at the end of the 1980s. This was due, in part, to R.E.M, a band with an MTV- and radio-friendly sound that appealed to fans across the musical spectrum. R.E.M. was founded in 1980 by singer Michael Stipe, guitarist Peter Buck, bassist Mike Mills, and drummer Bill Berry. All attended the University of Georgia in Athens, where the growing indie music scene helped propel a local new-wave band, the B-52s, to national fame in the early 1980s.

The B-52s' infectious mix of dance, surf, and punky rock music and humorous videos for hits like "Rock Lobster" and "Love Shack" made the group MTV favorites. The group's fame, however, was soon eclipsed by R.E.M., which built a substantial fan base playing local bars in Athens. R.E.M.'s first single, 1981's "Radio Free Europe," presented a classic mix of musical styles that would come to define alternative rock in later years. Although the band is often mocked for its unintelligible lyrics, this characteristic would become something of an R.E.M. trademark. Jason Crock, a contributor to the alternative music website Pitchfork, explains:

> [The song's] slashing chords may have had roots in punk, but the band replaced all their bile and angst with jangle, mystery, and inscrutability. . . . They aimed for a kind of danceable folk-punk . . . and the result was a little left of the mark, but it sounded like little else around . . . [and] altered the face of underground rock; it was the mumble heard 'round the world.[63]

After the release of their debut album, *Murmur*, R.E.M. followed the classic path to stardom for an indie band. Driven by a do-it-yourself spirit, the group toured relentlessly, playing big-city theaters and small-town dives. R.E.M. annually produced critically acclaimed albums like *Fables of Reconstruction* and *Life's Rich Pageant*, which only sold a few hundred thousand copies.

R.E.M.'s slow climb to stardom ended in 1987, when they achieved widespread fame with the album *Document*, which produced two hit singles, "The One I Love" and "It's the End of the World as We Know It (And I Feel Fine)." With its rapid-fire lyrical delivery, dynamic beat, and catchy chorus, "It's the End of the Word" helped spark a back-to-the-garage movement that spawned dozens of indie bands, including the Pixies, Dinosaur Jr., and My Bloody Valentine.

By the time *Document* was released, R.E.M. videos had become favorites on the MTV show dedicated to alternative music, *120 Minutes*, which was launched in 1986. After touring for years, the group retired from the road in 1988 to concentrate on recording. Their records, such as *Out of Time* (1991) and *Automatic for the People* (1992), helped make R.E.M. one of the best-selling bands in the world. When the group returned to the stage in 1995, they were hailed by critics and fans as pioneers of the alternative music scene, which was at its peak of popularity.

Indie Is a Way of Life

When R.E.M. first formed at the beginning of the 1980s, there was no such thing as indie music. By the end of the decade, a new musical style called alternative had been created out of genres as diverse as metal, reggae, funk, punk, rock, and folk. Bands like the Meat Puppets created a unique alt-rock sound by stitching hard core to electronic noise,

Michael Stipe was one of the founders of R.E.M., one of the best selling alternative rock bands in history.

surf music, and a sort of cracked country psychedelic sound taken from the Grateful Dead. While such musical mash-ups made alternative rock difficult to define as a specific sound, they also created an atmosphere in which any new sounds could incubate and grow.

Anthropologist Wendy Fonarow studied this musical range and diversity of 1980s indie rock and acknowledged that the sound could be defined by various factors, such as short songs, guitar bands, and a do-it-yourself attitude. According to Fonarow, there is more to indie rock than meets the ears:

> For each of the general principles there have been bands that defy the conventions and are still considered indie. There are indie bands that top the mainstream charts, indie bands on major labels, indie bands with major distribution, indie bands that utilize complex studio-produced sounds that cannot be played live, and indie bands that make eight-minute songs. There are even a few indie bands that do not use a guitar. . . . [Rather] than a distinctive sound, fashion, mode of production, and performance style [alt-rock] is an ethos [culture], an attitude. Indie . . . is a way of life . . . being free from control, dependence, or interference.[64]

CHAPTER 4

The Golden Age of Grunge

I n a 1972 article in *Creem* magazine, rock critic Lester Bangs imagined a type of alternative band the public might embrace in the post-hippie era. With a healthy dose of acerbic humor, Bangs wrote that his fantasy band could be called the Kozmik Mystik Okkult Jujube Ragas or possibly Mumbo Jumbo Merlin Mush. Bangs wrote: "What do they sound like? Great! Grunge noise and mystikal studio abstractions . . . vocals and organ and other things quite [like the heavy metal pioneers] Deep Purple, and if you've got any sense of humor or no standards at all you'll love 'em."[65] While Bangs was actually lamenting the rise of gimmicky glam rock in the early 1970s, he was the first person to equate the heavy metal sound with the term *grunge*. At the time, most people used the word to describe something dirty or filthy. From his perch as America's premier rock critic, Bangs peered into the rock-and-roll future and imagined a sound so raw and gritty it would be utterly grungy.

Lester Bangs died of an accidental drug overdose in 1982. Had he survived a few more years, Bangs might have met Mark Arm, from the Seattle, Washington, group Green River and later Mudhoney. In 1987, Arm described his band's dirty guitar sound as grunge. It is unknown if Arm followed Lester Bangs, but the term *grunge* caught on in the media and was soon applied to the music of other regional Seattle bands like Nirvana, Soundgarden, and Pearl Jam.

"The Antithesis of Glitz"

Grunge music emerged in a region that launched garage rock in the 1960s. The Kingsmen, the Sonics, and Paul Revere and the Raiders all hailed from the Pacific Northwest. The metal master of the fuzz guitar, Jimi Hendrix, was from Seattle. The city also had a large hardcore community and was a regular stop for hard-core bands like Hüsker Dü and Black Flag. At the end of the 1980s, these musical influences came together to form the unique grunge sound.

The Seattle region is known today as a high-tech haven, home to the corporate headquarters of Microsoft, Amazon .com, Nintendo, and the ubiquitous coffee chain Starbucks. In the late 1980s, however, Starbucks was just a local coffee shop, the computer boom was in its infancy, and Amazon .com did not exist because the World Wide Web did not go online until 1993.

In this pre-Internet era, Seattle had an outsider status. It was the cloudiest and rainiest big city in the country and culturally and geographically isolated. As rock journalist Laura Singara explains:

> For jobless couch surfers nationwide, Seattle fit the bill as a fantasy locale for low-rent escapism. It existed almost out of time, distant from the hubs of go-go '80s culture. Its mix of logging yahoos, homesteading hippies . . . eggheads, and [antigovernment] libertarians made it the antithesis of glitz. People who wanted to make their own fun formed an artistic community in this mossy world.[66]

Sub Pop's Ultra-Loose Grunge

The small city of Olympia, Washington, about 70 miles to the south of Seattle, housed an even sleepier artistic community. Many of the artists were students at the progressive Evergreen State College. Evergreen was also home to the

Grunge Shines a Spotlight on Seattle

In 1993, due to the popularity of Nirvana and other regional bands, Seattle, Washington, and its grunge fashions were prominently featured in mainstream publications such as *Time*, *Entertainment Weekly*, *USA Today*, and *Rolling Stone*. A *New York Times* article noted the plethora of coffee shops and small independent beer breweries in the city and stated grunge music was inspired by Seattle's three principle drugs—espresso, beer, and heroin.

Driven by the media hype, grunge fans across the country adopted the fashions worn by Seattle musicians. This included long, stringy hair, plaid or striped flannel shirts, Doc Marten boots, and knit hats. While Seattleites wore these cheap clothes to stay warm and dry in a rainy climate, grunge styles were soon featured at pricey fashion shows. A Perry Ellis collection displayed models in silk plaid shirts, while a *Vogue* fashion spread called "Grunge and Glory" featured grungy outfits that cost thousands of dollars.

community radio station KAOS, known for its extensive collection of indie records.

One student at Evergreen, Bruce Pavitt, began printing a fanzine called *Subterranean Pop* at the school in 1979. The zine, which soon shortened its name to the catchier *Sub Pop*, covered the American alternative music scene. While some early issues of the magazine were printed, others were just music cassettes—mix tapes filled with music by regional acts.

Pavitt moved to Seattle and used his popular zine connections to the national indie scene to advance his own music label. In 1986, Pavitt joined with musician and college radio DJ Jonathan Poneman to create Sub Pop Records. The following year, Sub Pop released recordings by two seminal Seattle grunge bands, Green River and Soundgarden.

Poneman and Pavitt tapped into the indie community's love of humor to promote Sub Pop. When the Green River album *Dry as a Bone* was released, for example, it was advertised as "ultra-loose grunge that destroyed the morals of a generation."[67] The company also distributed its music through the Sub Pop Singles Club. Fans paid an annual subscription to the club and received singles in the mail every month.

Three Guys Sound Like Nine

In November 1988, the first record shipped through the Sub Pop Singles Club was "Love Buzz," a cover tune by a little-known band called Nirvana. Nirvana had played its second gig in the KAOS studios, broadcast on April 17, 1987. The grunge group also performed at various Olympia venues for the Evergreen student community organization.

The single was a cover of a 1969 one-hit wonder by the Dutch rock band Shocking Blue. At the hands of Nirvana, the song was classic Seattle grunge, filled with thick, muddy, distorted guitar textures blended with punk rock rhythms and attitude. The buzz from "Love Buzz" helped Nirvana land a steady stream of gigs from Olympia to Seattle.

Nirvana was formed in 1987 by singer/guitarist Kurt Cobain and bassist Krist Novoselic. They played with a rotating cast of drummers including Chad Channing and Dale Crover of the punk group the Melvins. By the end of 1988, Nirvana was a local legend. Zine journalist and Sub Pop employee Jeff Gilbert describes the scene at an Olympia show:

> Three guys making a sound that totally belied the band members. I mean, how do three guys sound like nine? It came from attitude, power, volume. . . . You hit that first note—Kurt would do a power chord, and the drums were starting to smack around a bit, and the bass would rumble for a minute. And then in one second, it would all come together, and just explode. It was like a lightning bolt hit. You saw more feet than hands in the air because people [in the audience] would go upside down.[68]

Nirvana released their first album, *Bleach*, on Sub Pop in June 1989. The group had recorded the album over the course of one week at the cost of $600, an astoundingly small amount for any record. *Bleach* sold more than thirty-five thousand copies and rescued Sub Pop from near bankruptcy. The company issued a press release for *Bleach* written in typical Sub Pop ironic style: "Hypnotic and righteous heaviness from these Olympia pop stars. They're young, they own their own van, and they're going to make us rich!"[69]

Like countless alternative rock bands before them, Nirvana went on a DIY summer road tour of the country in 1989. The band played packed houses of moshers and crowd surfers and slept in their van or on floors and couches offered by fans. Backed by their record label, Nirvana was even able to visit Europe in the fall, playing London, England; Berlin, Germany; Rome, Italy; and other cities.

In 1993, Kurt Cobain (left) and Dave Grohl of Nirvana taped MTV Live and Loud: Nirvana Performs Live *in Seattle.*

Despite the excitement of travel, all was not well. Nirvana was forced to share their tour van with another touring group, placing nine musicians packed shoulder-to-shoulder in a vehicle loaded down with heavy sound equipment and instruments. Someone was always carsick, and Cobain had chronic stomach pains and was ill most of the time. Tired and sick, members of Nirvana vented their frustrations on stage, shooting fire extinguishers into the crowds and breaking guitars and drums. At one point, Cobain climbed a tall speaker stack and threatened to jump before he was coaxed down by Novoselic.

Nirvana's Number One

After Nirvana returned home from Europe, the group began writing songs for their next album while continuing a grueling touring schedule. By this time, Cobain was unhappy with Channing's drumming. He was replaced in 1990 by Dave Grohl, a drummer who had previously played with the punk group Scream. Grohl's hard-hitting style added a new element of excitement to Nirvana's grunge sound.

By the end of 1990, Nirvana was so popular in the Seattle region that major record labels were checking out the band's concerts. In 1991, Nirvana signed with DGC, part of Geffen Records, and traveled to the Los Angeles area to record its second album, *Nevermind*. DGC gave the group a budget of $65,000 to make the record, more than a hundred times the cost of *Bleach*. The label planned to sell 250,000 copies of *Nevermind*, with sales led by the single "Smells Like Teen Spirit."

When the music video of "Teen Spirit" debuted on MTV's *120 Minutes*, all the copies of *Nevermind* sold out instantly. The video showed a gloomy high school gym packed with students in bleachers. As Nirvana plays the song, the crowd gets rowdy and, by the third verse, they are crowd surfing, stealing the band's instruments, and creating general mayhem.

The song "Smells Like Teen Spirit" was so popular *Nevermind* quickly climbed into the *Billboard* Top 40 album charts, hitting number one in January 1992, displacing Michael Jackson's *Dangerous*. The album also topped the charts in Canada, Ireland, Spain, and France and hit number seven in the United Kingdom. By this time, *Nevermind* was selling 400,000 copies a week in the United States alone.

Cobain had become the hottest new rock star in the world virtually overnight, but he was not happy. In addition to suffering from bouts of debilitating mental depression, Cobain held an abiding belief in musical authenticity, anticommercialism, and anticonsumerism. Cobain did not want to become another overexposed MTV superstar like Michael Jackson. In addition, his severe stomach problems continued, causing him to try heroin as a cure—a decision he came to regret.

The Moody Sound of Seattle

The popularity of *Nevermind* took the regional sound of grunge worldwide and made unlikely superstars out of bands like Pearl Jam, Alice in Chains, and Soundgarden. These bands did not all sound like Nirvana, nor did they sound like one another, but they did have similar roots. The grunge style was created by less than a hundred musicians who were all influenced by punk, hard core, and heavy metal from earlier decades. As Sub Pop producer Jack Endino states, grunge is "seventies-influenced, sloweddown punk music."[70] However, several musical elements separate grunge from punk and metal. One key element of grunge can be traced to the types of guitar chords used in the songs. In music theory, a chord, made up of three notes played simultaneously, can be a major or minor chord. Most popular rock acts primarily use major chords in their songs. Chords in a major key suggest cheeriness, intensity, and excitement.

Grunge bands tend to use moody-sounding minor chords. These chords, like Seattle's heavy clouds, can evoke feelings of sadness, anxiety, or concern. When grunge guitarists strum minor chords on instruments filtered with fuzz tone distortion, the music creates a sludgy dissonance that lies at the heart of the grunge sound.

Wah-Wah and Tuning

The Seattle sound also features a unique use of the wah-wah pedal. Grunge lead guitarists, such as Kim Thayil of Soundgarden and Mike McCready of Pearl Jam, borrowed several tricks from early heavy metal guitarists like Jimi Hendrix. Both grunge players featured the wah-wah foot pedal, which, as its name implies, gives a wah-wah sound to the guitar. When a guitarist pushes the pedal back and forth quickly, it bends the tone between extreme treble and heavy bass, creating a wah-wah sound. When left in the bass position, the wah-wah pedal gives the guitar a deep, murky sound.

Another technique popular among Seattle grunge players involved unusual guitar tunings. Grunge guitarists often detuned their guitars from a standard pitch to a lower pitch. When guitar strings are loosened, it gives the instrument an extreme low-end sound not commonly heard in pop music. The dropped tuning technique was widely used by rhythm guitarist Stone Gossard of Pearl Jam, Jerry Cantrell of Alice in Chains, and Kurt Cobain on *Nevermind*. The use of un-

Pearl Jam's Stone Gossard, left, and Eddie Vedder perform at Lollapalooza in 1992.

usual guitar tunings in rock did not originate in Seattle, but it was unusual that an entire group of bands in a single region used similar tuning techniques to obtain a specific sound.

Lollapalooza's Alternative Nation

During the 1990s, the Seattle grunge sound was at the center of a social phenomena called alternative culture. This culture spawned alternative fashions, alternative films, alternative books, and even an MTV music video show called *Alternative Nation*. The Lollapalooza music festival, which was first held in 1991, was ground zero for the alternative cultural movement.

Lollapalooza featured dozens of acts that played various alternative genres, including hip hop, grunge, post-punk, thrash, and industrial noise. The festival was very popular among a group of young people labeled by the media with the punkish name Generation X. Gen Xers, sometimes referred to as the children of hippies, were part of the approximately 46 million babies born between 1965 and 1980. Alternative rock is the sound of Gen X, a generation that also popularized tattoos, body piercing, moshing, skateboarding, and extreme sports. The darker side of the Alternative Nation could be heard in the lyrics of autobiographical songs about suicide, sexual abuse, psychological disorders, diseases, and drug addiction.

Lollapalooza ran annually and helped keep the public attuned to alternative culture. From 1991 through 1997, the festival lineup was a who's who of popular alt-rock acts, including Jane's Addiction, the Red Hot Chili Peppers, Nine Inch Nails, Pearl Jam, A Tribe Called Quest, Rage Against the Machine, Moby, Beck, Sonic Youth, Tool, and KoЯn. Pitchfork editor Chris Dahlen cynically explains the impact of Lollapalooza:

> Lollapalooza taught Generation X the power of choice—the choice to enjoy any genre, to follow any movement that had a good pamphlet or a cute activist at the signup table, [and] to pierce any part of your body. . . . There was no [overall political] movement—

Red Hot and Chili

The Los Angeles, California–based Red Hot Chili Peppers were one of the most successful alternative rock acts of the 1990s and remained popular in the twenty-first century. The group was formed by two high school friends, Anthony Kiedis (vocals) and Michael "Flea" Balzary (bass). The Red Hot Chili Peppers was among the first alternative rock bands to mix rock, rap, funk, and hard-core sounds inspired by Black Flag. By doing so, band members created an exhilarating new musical style of rocking punk funk that drove audiences wild at their explosive live shows.

During the mid-1980s, the Red Hot Chili Peppers featured a rotating cast of drummers and guitarists. After producing several critically acclaimed but slow-selling albums, the band released *Blood Sugar Sex Magik* in 1991. Driven by MTV videos of "Under a Bridge" and "Give It Away," *Blood Sugar Sex Magik* sold an amazing 7 million copies. Despite their success, hard drugs and changing personnel prevented the band from producing another megahit until 1999, when *Californication* was released. The record, which mixes power ballads and frenzied rap-rock, eventually sold more than 15 million copies, making it one of the most successful alt-rock records of the decade.

just a celebration of options that were exploding even before the World Wide Web gave everyone a virtual Lollapalooza that ran year-round.[71]

Cobain Burns Out

Due in part to Lollapalooza and MTV, grunge music was the sound of teenage America in the early 1990s. Pearl Jam's 1992 debut album, *Ten*, hit number two on the *Billboard* charts and produced three hit singles: "Alive," "Even Flow," and "Jeremy." Soundgarden's third album, *Badmotorfinger*, was one among the one hundred top-selling albums of the year.

While grunge culture spread across the planet, the band at the center of movement was out of commission. Nirvana only played thirty-five concerts in 1992 and did little rehearsing or recording. Band members were fighting over money and not even living in the same state. Cobain had married punk rocker Courtney Love of the band Hole that February. Like Cobain, Love was a heroin user, and the couple's stormy relationship and the media interest in their newborn daughter made bigger headlines than Nirvana's music.

As Cobain's life was spinning out of control, Nirvana recorded its third studio album, *In Utero*, in February 1993. Cobain's gloomy thoughts were revealed with lyrics that referred to suicide, rape, insanity, depression, abortion, and various bodily functions. When *In Utero* was released in September, it debuted at number one and received widespread acclaim in the music press. Nirvana followed the album's release with a sold-out world tour and a highly praised acoustic performance on *MTV Unplugged*.

In March of 1994, while Nirvana was on tour in Rome, Cobain was rushed to the hospital after mixing alcohol with "roofies," the powerful prescription drug Rohypnol. The rest of the tour was canceled as friends held a drug intervention and convinced Cobain to seek treatment for his continuing heroin addiction. He only stayed in the rehab clinic for seven days. On April 8, 1994, in a haze of heroin, the twenty-seven-year-old Cobain killed himself with a shotgun blast.

Cobain's death shocked millions of people. Never before had anyone seen a chart-topping musician commit suicide at the peak of his career. Cobain's picture appeared on the front page of nearly every magazine and newspaper in North America and Europe. A vigil organized in Seattle the day after his death attracted about ten thousand fans. During the vigil, Love read Cobain's scrawled suicide note aloud to the mourners. In the note, Cobain tries to justify his suicide to his fans:

> I haven't felt the excitement of listening to as well as creating music along with reading and writing for too many years now. I feel guilty beyond words about these things. . . . The fact is, I can't fool you, any one of you. It simply isn't fair to you or me. . . . Thank you all from the pit of my burning, nauseous stomach for your letters and concern during the past years. I'm too much of an erratic, moody baby! I don't have the passion

Nirvana drummer Dave Grohl formed the highly successful group the Foo Fighters after Kurt Cobain's death.

anymore, and so remember, it's better to burn out than to fade away.[72]

Live Through This

Many felt that Cobain's suicide also marked the sudden death of grunge music, but the sound did not burn out or fade away. Instead, grunge was absorbed, like so many other styles, into the general sound of alternative rock. The result was a cleaner, more commercial sound called post-grunge that was played by bands like Bush, Silverchair, and Creed.

One of the most successful post-grunge bands was formed by Nirvana drummer Dave Grohl, who founded the Foo Fighters soon after Kurt Cobain's death. Grohl played every instrument himself on his 1995 debut album, *Foo Fighters*, and the sound of the record came to define the post-grunge genre. Foo Fighters songs blend fuzzy grunge guitars and explosive drums with bright, accessible pop melodies and lyrics. Grohl went on to recruit other musicians to fill out the band. The Foo Fighters continue to release successful studio albums that are considered monuments to creativity and alt-rock innovation.

Courtney Love was working on Hole's second album, *Live Through This*, when Cobain died and released the record only days after his death. Despite questions about the timing, the album quickly went double platinum and was unanimously praised for its mix of punk, grunge, and pop rock music. Pitchfork called the songs on *Live Through This* "the most gut-wrenching performances of [Love's] career."[73]

Dreams of Smashing Pumpkins

When writing songs for *Live Through This*, Love worked closely with Billy Corgan, singer, songwriter, and guitarist for the Smashing Pumpkins. Corgan's band was among several alternative rock acts outside Seattle that benefited in the second part of the 1990s from the public embrace of grunge.

The Smashing Pumpkins was formed in 1981 in the Chicago, Illinois, suburb of Elk Grove Village by Corgan, James Iha (guitar), D'arcy Wretzky (bass), and Jimmy Chamberlin (drums). During the height of the grunge era, the Smashing Pumpkins achieved mainstream success with their second album, *Siamese Dreams*, which, according to rock music critic Jim DeRogatis, contains a "mix of gothic

The Industrial Sounds of Nine Inch Nails

Industrial music is an angry and abrasive melding of rock, punk, and electronic noise often set to pummeling dance beats. In the 1990s, Nine Inch Nails (NIN) brought industrial music to the mainstream. The band consists of a single member— singer / producer / multi-instrumentalist Trent Reznor. Nine Inch Nails is described by AllMusic staff writer Steve Huey:

> Unlike the vast majority of industrial artists, Reznor wrote melodic, traditionally structured songs where lyrics were a focal point. His pop instincts not only made the harsh electronic beats of industrial music easier to digest, but also put a human face on a style that usu-

ally tried to sound as mechanical as possible. . . . NIN built up a large alternative rock fan base right around the time of Nirvana's mainstream breakthrough [in 1992]. As a result, Reznor became a genuine star and his notoriously dark, brooding persona and provocateur instincts made him a . . . sex symbol for the '90s.

Steve Huey. "Nine Inch Nails," AllMusic, www.allmusic .com/artist/nine-inch-nails-p5033/biography, 2011.

Industrial music pioneer Trent Reznor performs as Nine Inch Nails at the 2005 Voodoo Music Experience in Memphis, Tennessee.

The Smashing Pumpkins benefited from the public embrace of grunge in the second part of the 1990s.

mope, arena bombast, and shred-metal/prog-rock virtuosity."[74]

In the aftermath of Cobain's death, many alternative rock fans were looking for a new voice to speak for their generation. Many chose Corgan, something he did not understand. As Corgan told *Spin* magazine in 1994: "I just find it puzzling. . . . I've never aspired to speak for anyone except your basic disaffected white suburban middle-class, which I guess is who everyone's talking about. . . . I apologize for not representing you well enough."[75]

After *Siamese Dreams* sold more than 6 million copies worldwide, the Smashing Pumpkins went to work on their most ambitious project, *Mellon Collie and the Infinite Sadness*. The epic concept album, with twenty-eight songs on two CDs, was more than two hours long. The songs fit into a broad theme meant to describe a typical day in the life of a disaffected teenager. The story is told through a wide range of music styles, including art rock, pop metal, industrial, and country punk. Jim DeRogatis reviewed the album for *Rolling Stone*:

> Musically, *Mellon Collie* solidifies Corgan's position as one of his generation's most ambitious songwriters— no one else in alternative rock's superstar stadium has attempted an album of such length, let alone scope, and it may even match [Pink Floyd's masterpiece] *The Wall* in its sonic accomplishments.[76]

The Smashing Pumpkins continued to release innovative, critically acclaimed albums throughout the 1990s. The group's singles were staples of alternative rock radio, but band members suffered problems common to many successful musicians: infighting and drug addiction. After the group's 2000 synthesizer-based album *MACHINA/The Machines of God* sold less than half a million copies, the Smashing Pumpkins broke up.

Beck performs with his band in California in 2006. Critics have contradictorily compared him to both Kurt Cobain and David Byrne.

Loser and "A Place to Go"

Billy Corgan was not the only alternative rocker to be compared to Kurt Cobain in 1994. Three weeks after the Nirvana singer shot himself, Beck's single "Loser" hit number ten on the *Billboard* charts. *Spin* magazine called Beck "a generation's consolation prize for the death of Kurt Cobain."[77] Despite this faint praise, Beck was poles apart from the anguished, angry Cobain. By utilizing ironic rapping, intelligent lyrics, white-boy funk grooves, and self-deprecating humor, Beck was closer to a 1990s version of art rocker David Byrne. In a 1996 interview, Beck positioned his music as the next step after grunge: "The nihilism of the whole grunge thing in America was just a purge. A purge of materialism and elitism that was the '80s. But ultimately there's a place to go after that."[78]

The Biggest Alt-Rock Band in the World

During the 1990s, U2 became the most famous alternative band in the world and one of the best-selling rock bands of all time. The Irish group from Dublin, Ireland, rose to fame in the 1980s with the classic alternative album *The Joshua Tree*. This record combined diverse styles of music including American blues, rock, and gospel and traditional Irish folk songs.

In 1990, U2 pushed further into alt-rock territory with *Achtung Baby*, an album produced by Brian Eno that mixed industrial music, hip-hop beats, and electronic dance music. Throughout the rest of the decade, U2 continued to push the boundaries of alternative rock, experimenting with each new record. The 1995 experimental album *Original Soundtracks 1* contained synthesizer-heavy songs, while the 1997 album *Pop* featured funky dance beats layered with sound samples, drum loops, and other computer wizardry.

Besides producing some of the most imitated alternative rock of the decade, U2 sold out stadiums and other huge concert venues worldwide. Unlike the many apathetic, nihilistic alt-rock tunes of the era, U2 songs contained political and social criticism along with spiritual messages. While inspiring their fans to volunteer for worthy causes, U2 raised tens of millions of dollars to alleviate starvation and help people in war-torn nations.

The place Beck proposed to go after grunge was his brand of alternative rock that combined a wider variety of sounds, including blues, rock, hip hop, and funk. He even paid tribute to country music, putting a banjo riff at the end of the brass-driven funk masterpiece "Sexx Laws" from the 1999 album *Midnight Vultures.*

On *Odelay*, Beck perfected his skills at sampling, the technique of using short segments of sounds from earlier recordings. The sax solo on "New Pollution" was pulled from a recording of the 1975 Joe Thomas song "Venus" and speeded up to double tempo. There is even classical music on "High 5," which contains a snippet of Franz Schubert's "Unfinished Symphony #8 in B Minor."

After *Odelay*, Beck continued to produce highly praised, multiplatinum albums such as *Mutations* (1998), *Sea Change* (2002), and *Guero* (2004). In 2010, Beck wrote several songs played by the fictional band Sex Bob-Omb in the hit movie *Scott Pilgrim vs. the World.*

A New Era

After the grunge music movement took off in the 1990s, the guiding philosophy for alt-rockers was to fight the all-powerful record companies and radio stations owned by large multinational corporations. With a culture of write-it-yourself, record-it-yourself, and promote-it-yourself, alt-rock bands sought the independence and freedom to follow their creative dreams.

Independent record labels put musicians in charge and took away the power record companies held for more than a century as gatekeepers to the consumer market. This allowed alt-rockers to concentrate on creating new sounds to reach fans directly. For some, this independence enforced the belief that at the end of the twentieth century, there was never a better time to be an alternative rock musician.

CHAPTER 5

Alt-Rock's Digital New Age

Between the rise of Nirvana in 1990 and the collapse of the Smashing Pumpkins in 2000, increasingly powerful personal computers (PCs) changed the way people created music. Computing power and hard-drive storage increased more than ten times during the decade. By 1999, the latest PCs could be loaded with drumbeats, sampling software, and music sequencers (sound recording programs). These developments in technology provided amateur and professional musicians with a near infinite palette of sounds to work with. Digital tools also gave rise to a new form of alternative music, synthesizer-based electronica performed by acts such as Prodigy, Moby, and the Chemical Brothers. In addition, electronic sounds were widely incorporated into traditional guitar-and-drum alt-rock bands including top acts like U2 and Oasis.

The digital revolution changed the way music was consumed. After launching in 1993, the explosive growth of the World Wide Web freed listeners from the standards imposed by FM radio. Any garage band with a PC and an Internet connection could stream song files from a Web page or send them out to listeners from New York to New Zealand.

With digital sampling, computerized recording, and Internet distribution, the world of alternative rock had changed immeasurably. However, alt-rock continued to be based on a do-it-yourself culture, and personal computers simply became an extension of that philosophy. Computers allowed the up-and-coming stars to record on a laptop for next to nothing in the kitchen, living room, or bedroom.

Peer-to-Peer

The growth of digital music production and promotion allowed countless alternative rockers to continue sidestepping major record labels in the late 1990s. Few could picture the music industry in a death spiral as a result of this revolution. Fewer still could imagine that a near fatal blow to the record business would come from Napster, a music-sharing software developed in a dorm room on a Dell laptop computer by a college kid named Shawn Fanning.

iPods and iTunes

In late 2001, Apple Computer introduced the iPod music player. Within two years, more than 2 million iPods were sold. By 2010, about one out of every twenty-two people on earth owned an iPod, after Apple sold about 297 million of the music players. The sleek new MP3 player made it extremely easy for fans to store and play stolen music.

Steve Jobs, founder and CEO of Apple, was sympathetic to the fact that most iPods were filled with illegally downloaded songs. He addressed the issue in a 2003 *Rolling Stone* interview: "Our position from the beginning has been that eighty percent of the people stealing music online don't really want to be thieves. . . . [Apple's position is:] We're gonna offer you a better experience . . . and it's only gonna cost you a dollar a song." Jobs opened the iTunes Store in April 2003, positioning it as a solution to illegal downloading.

Millions of iPod users were eager to use the legal alternative to stealing music. More than 1 million songs were sold through the iTunes Store within the first five days of operation. In a little over a year, more than 100 million songs were legally purchased from the iTunes Store, a number that increased to nearly 9 billion by 2009.

Quoted in Jeff Goddell. "Steve Jobs: The Rolling Stone Interview," *Rolling Stone*, www.rollingstone.com /news/story/5939600/steve_jobs_the_rolling_stone _interview/3, December 3, 2003.

In June 1999, Fanning was an eighteen-year-old student at Northeast University in Boston. While trying to devise a method to share his music with his friends, he invented the software program Napster. This program allowed peer-to-peer (P2P) music file sharing through the Internet. Napster users could type the name of a song into the program's search box and be downloading that tune in the MP3 file format within seconds for free.

The Napster software program quickly went viral, rapidly spreading from person to person across the globe. By January 2000, Napster claimed 150,000 users, who had access to 20 million songs. By early 2001, the number of Napster users exploded to more than 30 million. Forty percent of the users were college students in the United States, and 2.8 billion files per month were being downloaded worldwide.

Napster creator Shawn Fanning wears a Metallica T-shirt, mocking the band's lawsuit against him.

Hoping to fight the trend, the music business trade group the Recording Industry Association of America (RIAA) placed ads in music magazines with the message that downloading songs for free is illegal. The practice violates copyright laws that give artists and record companies the right to control the use and reproduction of original works. The RIAA sued Fanning for copyright infringement, and Napster was shut down in 2001. By then, though, second-generation P2P software was available on websites like Gnutella and Kazaa. The trend of downloading music for free continued, sending shock waves that rattled the record industry at its foundations. As CD sales plunged, record companies laid off personnel and record stores were closed.

Trafficking in Stolen Goods

Alternative rockers were divided over the rise of P2P networks. Established groups with substantial CD sales feared financial ruin if their fans chose to download their music for free. However, relatively unknown bands believed file sharing provided free exposure to new fans, which would be beneficial in the long run.

The thrash metal pioneers Metallica were among those who opposed free file sharing. In April 2000, Metallica drummer Lars Ulrich filed a lawsuit against Napster shortly after it went online. When Ulrich arrived at court in Los Angeles, he brought thirteen boxes containing lists of 335,435 Napster users who had illegally downloaded Metallica songs during a two-day period that March. Ulrich made a statement to the press: "It is sickening that our art is being traded like a commodity rather than the art that it is. This is about taking something that doesn't belong to you. The trading of such information is . . . trafficking in stolen goods."[79]

Whatever his motives, Ulrich alienated some dedicated Metallica fans. Numerous critics in fanzines and on the web portrayed Metallica members as selfish, out-of-touch rock stars. Many began spelling Ulrich's name with a dollar sign—Lar$. Ulrich was even booed at the 2000 MTV Music Video Awards.

"Art-Rock Drama"

In contrast to Metallica, the British group Radiohead, which was relatively unknown in 2000, found a way to profit from the new digital developments. Radiohead consists of Thom Yorke (vocals, guitars, keyboards), Jonny Greenwood (guitars, keyboards), Ed O'Brien (guitars), Colin Greenwood (bass, synthesizers), and Phil Selway (drums). The group rose to fame in England in the 1990s producing unique albums that combined electronic sound effects with slow-tempo ballads and swirling guitar textures, sudden tempo changes, and screaming heavy metal interludes. Yorke's wispy, quivery falsetto broke through the noise, providing contrasting emotions. Rock journalist Will Hermes calls Radiohead's music "perfumed high-romanticism, art-rock drama, [and] suburban computer-age dread."[80]

Radiohead's critically acclaimed third album, *OK Computer* (1997), was the band's first number one in the United Kingdom. The melodic songs helped the album reach number twenty-one in the United States and earned the band its first Grammy nomination.

Ed O'Brien, Thom Yorke, and Jonny Greenwood of Radiohead in concert in 2008 in Amsterdam. Their highly experimental sound has been commercially successful.

Sales of *OK Computer* were generated by buzz on alternative rock websites. When Radiohead was preparing to release its next album, *Kid A*, in October 1999, the Internet helped boost sales once again, this time by accident. In the months before the album was released, songs from *Kid A* began appearing on Napster. But rather than harm Radiohead's sales, the illegal previews brought massive attention to *Kid A*.

Even though the music was largely experimental, filled with eerie avant-garde electronica and noncommercial underground sounds, *Kid A* debuted at number one in both the United States and the United Kingdom. The record received a Grammy for Best Alternative Album, inspired *Spin* to name Radiohead Band of the Year, and has achieved dozens of awards since its release. Capital/EMI's vice president of marketing, Rob Gordon, commented on the album's success: "We didn't use Napster. We wanted to keep [*Kid A*] off Napster. But when it went up, did it create more excitement, more enthusiasm? Absolutely."[81]

By 2007, Radiohead was a successful, internationally renowned alternative rock band. When the group decided to release its seventh album, *In Rainbows*, it bypassed its record label completely and made the record freely available on its website. Fans were asked to donate whatever amount they deemed appropriate. On the day of release, hundreds of thousands of downloads were reported for *In Rainbows*. The band did not provide sales figures for the album, but it is estimated that about one-third of the downloaders paid nothing, while the remaining two-thirds paid an average price of about $6. When *In Rainbows* was officially released on CD the following year, it sold more than 3 million copies in twelve months.

The White Stripes' New Rock Revolution

Radiohead's success with *In Rainbows* proved that some bands could thrive with free music downloads. Guitarist Jack White, of the White Stripes, took a different approach, writing, performing, producing, and marketing music at a frenzied pace to make his music pay.

The White Stripes was a duo from Detroit, Michigan,

Meg White and Jack White of the White Stripes used creative marketing strategies to sell albums in an age of illegal downloading.

formed in 1997 by White and his wife, drummer Meg White. As one of the few bands composed solely of a guitarist and drummer, the White Stripes gained immediate attention for their stripped-down sound that combined garage rock, blues, and punk.

When the White Stripes released their third album, *White Blood Cells*, in 2001, the album was a smash hit, widely praised by critics and fans. Dressed in their candy cane outfits—Jack in red and Meg in white—the duo proved to be eye candy for MTV. The group's clever music video for "Fell In Love with a Girl," which re-created band members from Lego building blocks, was nominated for four MTV Video Awards, including Best Video of the Year.

Beyond their pleasing commercial image, the White Stripes were credited for reviving garage rock and even saving rock and roll. At the time, the music charts were dominated by teen idols like *NSYNC and Britney Spears and smooth rappers like Sean "Puff Daddy" Combs. In this cultural climate, the mainstream press was instantly attracted to Jack White's mix of roots blues, heavy Led Zeppelin power chords, Bob Dylan folk styles, and Beatlesque jangle rock. Jack's virtuoso guitar playing was driven by Meg's minimalist drumming, which was influenced by Mo Tucker of the Velvet Underground. By the time the White Stripes released their platinum album *Elephant* in 2003, the group had been

Jack White Loves Vinyl

Jack White, formerly of the White Stripes, updated alt-rock for the new millennium with his virtuoso guitar playing, his ability to reference traditional styles like blues and rockabilly, and his do-it-yourself business sense. White's Third Man Records also spearheaded a vinyl revival, releasing twenty-first-century alt-rock music on vinyl records, a format that went out of style in the 1980s.

Long before compact discs (CDs) were available, vinyl records dominated music sales for decades. Rock and roll was introduced to the world in the 1950s on 45 rpm (revolutions per minute) vinyl singles and long-playing (LP) vinyl albums. Sales of vinyl plunged in 1990, but some music lovers were unhappy with this development. They felt that vinyl records had a warmer "living" sound that was better than digital recordings.

Vinyl does have its drawbacks. Dust and scratches produce audio pops, crackles, and skips that interfere with listening enjoyment. Despite the imperfections, White was among those who preferred the vinyl sound, and his international success allowed him to produce and sell high-quality vinyl records through Third Man Records. White discovered that collectors were eager to buy his limited-edition, brightly colored vinyl. White's vinyl revival is behind the motto of Third Man Records: "Your Turntable's Not Dead."

fondly profiled in *Rolling Stone*, *Time*, *The New Yorker*, and *Entertainment Weekly*.

Jack and Meg White divorced in 2005 but continued to play together for five more years. During that period, Jack proved to be a master at making money in a world of illegal downloads. In 2006, the White Stripes recorded an avant-garde orchestral album, called *Aluminum*, which probably would not have attracted as many buyers as the group's previous records. To build excitement, the band announced that

Aluminum would be released in limited editions on a CD and on old-style vinyl records. Each numbered album was signed by the White Stripes. The excitement generated by this unique release helped *Aluminum* sell out within days.

Jack White was at the center of a music marketing whirlwind throughout the rest of the decade. The White Stripes released a film of their 2007 Canadian concert tour called *Under Great White Northern Lights*. The film was part of an expensive limited-edition boxed set that included a DVD and a sound track album on CD and vinyl.

In 2009, White formed another group called Dead Weather, an alt-rock supergroup that consisted of musicians from the groups the Kills, Queens of the Stone Age, and the Raconteurs. In order to market Dead Weather and other alternative rock groups, White opened the Third Man Records store in Nashville, Tennessee, in 2009. Third Man Records is a record label, record store, and performance venue where the company's bands play and record. Third Man Records has signed dozens of bands and rereleased early White Stripes albums on vinyl.

The White Stripes broke up in 2010, but Jack White continued as a solo performer, television and movie personality, and record label executive. While White Stripes albums have been illegally downloaded by the millions, White is thriving in a tough business, tapping his talents, working relentlessly, and cleverly marketing his music.

Alternative Nation, Version 2.0

The success of the White Stripes was credited with kicking off what *Entertainment Weekly* labeled "Alternative Nation, Version 2.0."[82] The article pointed out that Jack White's success helped boost the careers of formerly obscure alt-rockers like Franz Ferdinand, the Strokes, and the Yeah Yeah Yeahs. These groups, at the forefront of what was called a new rock revolution, tapped into 1980s-style art rock, punk, and new wave for inspiration. Critic Craig McLean of London's *Sunday Times* raved about the Yeah Yeah Yeahs:

> When you're America's coolest group . . . you don't do many things the normal way. You make eye-blistering

videos, perform roof-rattling art-punk gigs and, in the shape of third album *It's Blitz!*, pump out thrillingly innovative electro-pop dance songs that pound another hefty nail into the coffin of tired old indie-guitar music.[83]

McLean was referring to the tired old indie-guitar music of bands like Limp Bizkit and Creed, which were dominating the rock radio airwaves at the time. These groups sold millions of records and earned countless awards by combining metal, rap, and cleaned-up post-grunge music. Despite the fact that Creed was one of the most successful bands in rock history, it was repeatedly condemned for imitating Alice in Chains and other Seattle grunge rockers. As *Spin* critic David Marchese writes, Creed's "music was unremarkable—[a] plodding muscle-bound reworking of Pearl Jam, with all of that older band's warmth and psychological intensity replaced by chest-beating bravado and bland . . . lyrics."[84]

Although Creed sold 35 million records, the group failed to connect with younger audiences on MTV. Hoping to draw in a younger demographic, MTV took a chance on videos by relatively unknown Alt-Nation 2.0 groups like Modest Mouse, Death Cab for Cutie, and the Killers. MTV fans responded positively to the new sounds and began requesting videos by the new rockers. Sub Pop Records founder Jonathan Poneman explains the phenomenon: "A generational shift is taking place. People want smart, thoughtful, passion-filled music again."[85]

"Supersonic Hardcore Bubblegum Brats"

With illegal downloading a fact of life for alternative rockers, the Berkeley, California–based band Green Day reacted to the phenomenon in an unusual way. In 2004, fans could purchase five blank, recordable CDs (CD-Rs) from the Green Day website for $7.99. The CD-Rs were branded with the artwork from each of Green Day's five albums. The band's label, Warner Bros., explained the idea. Fans who downloaded Green Day albums from iTunes could burn them onto the branded CD-Rs. Left unsaid was the fact

Green Day's music is sometimes called post-punk, music that incorporates pop and rock elements.

that Green Day's albums were widely available for free on P2P websites and that the discs could also be used to burn pirated albums, even those by other groups. Green Day drummer Tré Cool said he did not care how people used the CD-Rs: "If you can't beat people, join them. If people don't want to pay for music, that's their own deal. I'm not going to tell them they're bad or sit here and [complain] about it and take people to court. They're going to do it anyway."[86]

Green Day viewed the promotion as one more way the band could make money from their music, but by that time members of Green Day were all very rich. The band burst onto the alt-rock scene in the early 1990s, playing a matchless blend of pop, rock, and punk sometimes called new punk or post-punk. Cool, along with lead singer Billie Joe Armstrong and bassist Mike Dirnt, toured constantly in

1992 and 1993, building a fan base in the United States and Europe. When Green Day released its 1994 album *Dookie*, fans snapped up the album, which eventually sold 10 million copies worldwide. Videos of the *Dookie* singles "Longview" and "When I Come Around" saturated MTV's airwaves and made Green Day punk-pop superstars. In 1995, British zine critic Sylvie Simmons explained why Green Day was a hit on both sides of the Atlantic Ocean:

> So what kind of band are they? In a nutshell: supersonic hardcore bubblegum brats. A bright, crazy, brilliant cartoon with fast, tight, good-time songs. Songs about important things in life: beer, birds [girls], boredom, dope . . . television. . . . They're exactly what they intended to be—punk rock through a dayglo California blender that's more skateboards than Sex Pistols, more sex than social conscience.[87]

Green Day's supersonic sound, marked by Armstrong's fast down strum on his electric guitar and Cool's over-the-top drumming, was credited with reviving punk rock for a new generation. While some hard-core fans derided the sound as too poppy, calling it mall punk, by 2000 Green Day had grossed millions of dollars in record sales, merchandise, performance fees, and music publishing royalties.

Rock Is Supposed to Be Dangerous

Billie Joe Armstrong continued to write songs that were alternately sincere, scathing, and humorous. As music journalist Matt Diehl writes, Green Day's "combination of sensitive singer-songwriter idealism and fist-pumping guitar crunch . . . [is] imbued with a new hope. And . . . Green Day's classic punk moves sounded fresh."[88] However, Green Day's follow-up albums *Nimrod* and *Warning* sold poorly compared to *Dookie*. By 2000, the group's popularity had fallen to the point that Green Day was touring as an opening act for the punk pop group Blink-182, whose 2001 album *Take Off Your Pants and Jacket* had recently gone double platinum.

Green Day's fading destiny reversed during the turbulent years of the early twenty-first century. A series of stunning events provided Armstrong with inspirational songwriting material. The new songs refreshed the band's music and helped make the group more relevant to listeners. Armstrong began writing songs heavy with political and social commentary in 2001, when conservative Republican George W. Bush became president after a highly divisive election. On September 11, 2001, eight months after Bush was sworn in, terrorists flew jets into the World Trade Center in New York City and the Pentagon in Washington, D.C. The United States launched a worldwide war on terror in the aftermath, invading Iraq in 2003. Armstrong was extremely critical of the president, his followers, and the climate of fear that seemed to grip the entire nation. The result was the 2004 album *American Idiot*, a rock opera in which all the songs are interrelated and tell a story.

American Idiot is a cutting portrait of twenty-first-century American life. According to punk rock journalist Ben Meyers, Green Day sang about "a nation ruled by an idiot, misinformed by the media, and subjugated to a worldwide 'redneck agenda,' all seen through the eyes of an everyman [named Jesus of Suburbia]."[89] The album takes listeners through shopping malls, suburban streets, and barrooms while introducing a cast of characters that includes St. Jimmy, Whatsername, and President Gasman. Armstrong explained how the content of *American Idiot* was inspired by his punk roots:

> We live in times of terror and now is the time to speak out. We wanted to face danger, put it on the line and tell people what we think. Rock 'n' roll is supposed to be dangerous, that's where we come from. For us, our education wasn't what we learned in school, it was what we learned on Dead Kennedys records, Clash records. We're a part of that.[90]

American Idiot was released with a drawing of a bloody cartoon hand holding a heart-shaped hand grenade. The album sold more than 14 million copies, won numerous awards, and produced five chart-topping singles, including "Boulevard of Broken Dreams" and "Wake Me Up When September Ends." Music videos of the songs received heavy airplay.

An Amazing Comeback

More important than sales figures and receiving MTV video awards, *American Idiot* launched a remarkable comeback for Green Day, which played 150 concerts throughout the world in 2005. Billie Joe Armstrong commented on this new era for his band: "I think what *American Idiot* has done for us is really change our own history in a lot of ways. . . . It created a new future for us. It made all our albums since *Dookie* make sense for people who weren't really up to speed with what we were doing."[91]

In 2009, Green Day released its second rock opera, *21st Century Breakdown*, which was broken up into three acts meant to be commentaries on American life: "Heroes and Cons," "Charlatans and Saints," and "Horseshoes and Handgrenades." In addition to selling the album through traditional means, the group released a vinyl edition limited to only three thousand copies, which consisted of three short records, each containing one act of the rock opera.

While *21st Century Breakdown* sold only about 4 million copies, Green Day continued to remain in the news when they created *American Idiot: The Musical*. The stage play, initially produced by the Berkeley Repertory Theater in Berkeley, California, in 2009, began a sold-out run on Broadway in April 2010. In 2011, there was speculation the play might be turned into a movie. Meanwhile, Green Day continued to maximize their profits, lending their name to the video game *Green Day: Rock Band*, which allows players to simulate performances of songs from *Dookie*, *American Idiot*, and *21st Century Breakdown*. Between 1995 and 2011, music fans purchased 65 million albums by Green Day. This made them the most popular punk band of the era, prompting bassist Mike Dirnt to comment in 2005: "It makes me extremely proud to make punk rock the biggest music in the world right now."[92]

Genre Grab Bags

While Green Day's post-punk sound dominated the charts in the 2000s, countless experimental styles of alternative rock also emerged during the era. Harkening back to the

The Go! Team perform their unique blend of music at the SXSW Film and Music Festival in Austin, Texas, in 2006.

early era of indie rock, the sounds were unique, diverse, and completely noncommercial. The duo known as the Books, for example, released several albums on a German independent label, including *Thought For Food* and *The Lemon of Pink*. Songs by the Books feature snippets of cello, violin, banjo, and detuned acoustic guitar. These are mixed into cut-and-paste sound samples that include electronic noises, nonsense phrases, melodic singing, laughing, whistling, voice collages, bubbles, and unidentifiable noises.

Another inventive band, the British sextet the Go! Team, created truly bizarre sound-mixing tracks with samples of syrupy 1960s orchestral sound tracks backed by garage rock drumming. The group's debut album, *Thunder, Lightning, Strike*, was listed as number eight on Pitchfork's top ten albums of the year in 2004.

The Go! Team was founded by multi-instrumentalist Ian Parton, who began his career as a filmmaker. When compil-

Toying with the Lines Between Genres

Illegal music downloads and less-profitable online music sales have hurt the music industry but have provided great benefits for alternative rock fans. Pitchfork editor-in-chief Scott Plagenhoef explains:

For listeners . . . the Internet has opened countless doors. Rather than have to hunt for months (if not years) to locate a record, much of the history of pop music is now at our fingertips. And, at the beginning, as Napster exploded, this was undoubtedly a positive thing. Music fans from around the globe, and with different sensibilities and biases, gathered online to seek out music, acquire it, and discuss it. New conversations began, conventional wisdom was challenged, and a younger and more varied set of voices evangelized about everything from the usual sacred cows to Southern hip-hop, metal, noise . . . dance-punk, and chart pop.

Fortunately, too, there were a lot of conversations worth having. From the . . . racial-line blurring rhymes of Eminem to the New Rock Revolution of the Strokes and the White Stripes to Radiohead's electronic frontiersmanship to Timbaland and the Neptunes' merging of the avant-garde and pop, it was a good time to have access to a multitude of sounds. The eclecticism paid off: Chart music was as creatively rich as . . . [artists] toyed with the lines between the genres.

Scott Plagenhoef and Ryan Schreiber, eds. *The Pitchfork 500*. New York: Simon & Schuster, 2008, p. 158.

ing sounds for his album, Parton scoured the dusty shelves of thrift shops, purchasing scratchy old records that could be sampled.

"The Power Is On," a song from *Thunder, Lightning, Strike*, was compiled using the thrift store vinyl. Used in the sound track for the Drew Barrymore film *Whip It*, "The Power Is On" is an eardrum-splitting mash up of jump rope chants, cheerleaders cheering, sound tracks from educational films, and show tunes. Pitchfork managing editor Mark Richardson fondly analyzes the Go! Team's sound:

Often such genre grab-bags end up chaotic failures, but Parton [mashes them together] adeptly . . . conjuring up a piano thunderstorm, shadowboxing with horn-section blasts, and crusting it all with shrieking guitar abuse. Instead of coasting on empty, nostalgic button-pushing, Parton isolates the warm and unique properties of each sample, reconstituting it as a sun-faded historical document of a musical era that never existed. Anyone can pull that ironic T-shirt off the thrift store racks, but it takes a pro to piece together the whole outfit.[93]

Arcade Fire's Funeral

Regine Chassagne, left, and Win Butler of Arcade Fire perform with cinematic style in San Francisco in 2011.

Elements of Ian Parton's theatrical sounds and mixed instrumental blasts can be heard in the cinematic music of Arcade Fire. The seven-piece Montreal, Canada–based band cranks out a huge orchestral sound with violins, violas, cellos, horns, harps, guitars, organs, pianos, synthesizers, accordions, xylophones, recorders, percussion, bass,

and drums. These instruments are not combined in a traditional orchestral manner. *Chicago Tribune* reporter Robert Mitchum describes the Arcade Fire sound while analyzing the song "Neighborhood #1 (Tunnels)" from the band's 2004 album *Funeral*:

> Arcade Fire melodrama is anything but mellow. . . . [Lead singer] Win Butler's quaver suits the diary-entry lyrics, and the song just keeps upping the ante: out-of-context disco-punk drums and xylophone, the sawed strings, and the "Chopsticks" like piano, all building to one of their many chorally cathartic finales. . . . [At] a time when rock music struggled to be emotional . . . Arcade Fire's all-out live approach was a much-needed alternative to simpering faux [fake] intimacy.[94]

Despite bleak lyrics that touched on the deaths of beloved family members, suicidal tendencies, jilted lovers, and apocalyptic disasters, *Funeral* won dozens of music industry and media awards. After the success of the album, Arcade Fire continued to build an audience, playing on television, appearing at large music events such as the Coachella Valley Music and Arts Festival, and even warming up for the powerhouse U2 when they appeared in Canada in 2005. By the time Arcade Fire's second album, *Neon Bible*, was released in 2007, the band had generated considerable worldwide marketing buzz.

Neon Bible, which debuted at number two on the *Billboard* 200, followed the same musical formula as *Funeral*, but the group created new moods by utilizing a military choir, pipe organs, and the occasional full orchestra. Throughout 2007 and early 2008, Arcade Fire toured constantly to promote *Neon Bible*, playing 122 shows in nineteen countries. Film footage from the Neon Bible tour was compiled into a film called *Miroir Noir*, made available on DVD and as a download from the band's website.

Arcade Fire released *The Suburbs* in 2010. Once again, critics and the public responded in an overwhelmingly positive manner. *The Suburbs* debuted at number one in the United Kingdom, the United States, and Canada, and was named best album of the year by the Grammys, the Canadian Juno Awards, and the U.K. BRIT Awards.

The Anguished World of Emo

In the early 2000s, emo music and fashions began attracting widespread attention in the media. Emo, or emotional hard-core music, is aimed at adolescents. The songs contain dramatic lyrics about dark moods, twisted emotions, and depressing feelings. Emo emerged from the early grunge movement in 1991. The Seattle, Washington–based group Sunny Day Real Estate was one of the originators of the sound. The group softened the hard edges of punk by adding melody, sweeping guitar sounds, and slower, sophisticated rhythms. Most important, the emo pioneers composed songs from the perspective of a tortured artist full of bitterness, frustration, and anguish.

Emo remained an underground phenomenon until the early 2000s, when the style surged in popularity due to word-of-mouth advertising. The albums *Bleed American* by Jimmy Eat World and *The Places You Have Come to Fear the Most* by Dashboard Confessional led to the mainstream acceptance of the sound. Beyond the music, emo subculture was at the center of a fashion boom. A typical emo male outfit consisted of skinny jeans, a tight T-shirt, black horn-rimmed glasses, and a studded belt. Rockers with long, side-swept bangs that covered one or both eyes were instantly identified as emo fans.

The Truth Is Alternative

Arcade Fire is another band with a unique indie sound that managed to cross over to pop music stardom. The group's songs unfold like movies on a screen and make people dance while addressing the soullessness of the suburbs, the mindlessness of modern culture, and even death and destruction. As Pitchfork critic Ian Cohen writes, Arcade Fire's music centers on "modern disillusionment and disappointment for people who can commiserate and return to fretting about their jobs and bank accounts once the house lights go up. . . . And that Arcade Fire can make such powerful art out of recognizing these moments makes our own existences feel worthy of documentation. . . . [The band] delivers a life-affirming message. . . . We're all in this together."[95]

Addressing modern disillusionment and disappointment has been the goal of alt-rockers since the punks first plugged in their guitars in the 1970s. Since then, every decade has produced its disaffected teenagers and angry musicians who strive to put real emotions and authentic feelings into words and sounds. The music might be called garage, punk, metal, grunge, or noise, but in a world dominated by cheesy mindless pop songs, music that presents a truthful point of view is often called alternative.

Perhaps the alt-rockers' love of irony can be traced to the fact that speaking the truth is called alternative, while synthetic pop music is called mainstream. Whatever the case, without alternative rock, the music of the past half-century would have been bland indeed. In a culture dominated by money, greed, and power, alternative rock doubtlessly helped save the sanity of millions with the message "we're all in this together." That point has been made by musicians since the 1960s and will doubtlessly remain vital well into the uncertain future.

NOTES

Introduction: Indies, Phonies, and Alts

1. Kaya Oakes. *Slanted and Enchanted*. New York: Henry Holt, 2009, p. 10.
2. Quoted in Nelson George and Daphne Carr, eds. *Best Music Writing 2008*. New York: Da Capo Press, 2008, p. 8.
3. Quoted in Eric Weisbard. "Nirvana," *Spin*, April 2004, p. 72.

Chapter 1: Garage Rockers and Proto-Punks

4. Jon Pareles. "A New Kind of Rock," www.nytimes.com/1989/03/05/arts/home-entertainment-recordings-soundings-a-new-kind-of-rock.html, March 5, 1989.
5. Pareles. "A New Kind of Rock."
6. Quoted in Dave Marsh. *Louie Louie*. New York: Hyperion, 1993, p. 78.
7. Quoted in Marsh. *Louie Louie*, p. 103.
8. Marsh. *Louie Louie*, p. 114.
9. Quoted in Marsh. *Louie Louie*, p. 116.
10. Eric James Abbey. *Garage Rock*. Jefferson, NC: McFarland & Company, 2006, pp. 53–54.
11. Marsh. *Louie Louie*, p. 144.
12. Keith Richards. *Life*. New York: Little, Brown and Company, 2010, p. 54.
13. Richards. *Life*, p. 28.
14. Abbey. *Garage Rock*, p. 51.
15. Quoted in Nicholas Dawidoff. "Paul Simon's Restless Journey," *Rolling Stone*, May 13, 2011, p. 60.
16. David Fricke, Mikal Gilmore, et al. "The 70 Greatest Dylan Songs," *Rolling Stone*, May 26, 2011, p. 60.
17. Quoted in Fricke, Gilmore. "70 Greatest Dylan Songs," p. 54.
18. Quoted in Fricke, Gilmore. "70 Greatest Dylan Songs," p. 56.
19. Abbey. *Garage Rock*, p. 69.
20. Quoted in Zack Taylor. "American Beauty," Keno, www.keno.org/classic_rock/fan_album_reviews/the_dead.htm, October 22, 2007.
21. Stephen Thomas Erlewine. "In-A-Gadda-Da-Vida," AllMusic, www.allmusic.com/album/r9898, 2011.
22. Alan W. Pollack. "Notes on 'Helter Skelter,'" Soundscapes, www.icce.rug.nl/~soundscapes/DATABASES/AWP/hs.shtml, 1998.

Chapter 2: The Birth of Punk

23. Quoted in David Fricke. "Lou Reed," *Rolling Stone*, http://archive.rollingstone.com/Desktop#/19890504/36, 2011.

24. Scott D. Lipscomb. "Godfathers of Punk," University of Minnesota School of Music, www.lipscomb.umn.edu/rock/dizon_godfather_of_punk.htm, 2011.

25. Michael Sandlin. "Mo Tucker's Bio," www.spearedpeanut.com/tajmoehal/bio/moebio.html, 2003.

26. Chris Smith. *101 Albums That Changed Popular Music*. New York: Oxford University Press, 2009, pp. 45–46.

27. Quoted in Jonah Bayer. "Take A Walk On the Wild Side," Gibson, www.gibson.com/en-us/Lifestyle/Features/take-a-walk-on-the-wild-915, September 15, 2009.

28. Stephen Thomas Erlewine and Mark Deming. "The Stooges," iggypop.org, http://iggypop.org/stooges.html, April 26, 2008.

29. Marsh. *Louie Louie*, pp. 158.

30. Marsh. *Louie Louie*, pp. 158–159.

31. Larry Starr and Christopher Waterman. *American Popular Music from Minstrelsy to MTV*. New York: Oxford University Press, 2003, p. 370.

32. Patti Smith. *Just Kids*. New York: HarperCollins, 2010, pp. 175–176.

33. Quoted in Clinton Heylin. *Babylon's Burning: From Punk to Grunge*. New York: Canongate, 2007, p. 16.

34. Quoted in Heylin. *Babylon's Burning*, p. 17.

35. Quoted in Debra Wolter, ed. *Punk: The Whole Story*. London: DK, 2006, p. 71.

36. Quoted in Nick Tosches. *The Nick Tosches Reader*. New York: De Capo Press, 2000, p. 77.

37. Quoted in Smith. *101 Albums*, p. 120.

38. Quoted in Wolter. *Punk*, p. 72.

39. Dee Dee Ramone and Veronica Kofman. *Lobotomy: Surviving the Ramones*. New York: Thunder Mouth Press, 2000, p. 54.

40. Quoted in Jim Bessman. "Meet Punk Gormandizer Hilly Kristal, Iconic Owner of CBGB," *Billboard*, June 1, 2002, p. 87.

41. Matt Diehl. *My So-Called Punk*. New York: St. Martin's Griffin, 2007, p. 10.

42. Quoted in Wolter. *Punk*, p. 54.

43. Quoted in Legs McNeil. *Please Kill Me: The Uncensored Oral History of Punk*. New York: Grove Press, 1996, p. 199.

44. Quoted in Wolter. *Punk*, p. 280.

45. Quoted in Diehl. *My So-Called Punk*, p. 12.

46. Quoted in Wolter. *Punk*, p. 280.

Chapter 3: Indie Is a Way of Life

47. Richard Cromelin. "Reinvention Through Music," *Los Angeles Times*, June 11, 2011, p. D9.

48. Quoted in Joe Levy, ed. *The 500 Greatest Albums Of All Time*. New York: Wenner Books, 2005, p. 25.

49. Oakes. *Slanted and Enchanted*,

pp. 45–46.

50. Steve Waksman. *This Ain't the Summer of Love*. Berkeley: University of California Press, 2009, p. 10.

51. Quoted in Heylin. *Babylon's Burning*, p. 541.

52. Quoted in Heylin. *Babylon's Burning*, p. 546.

53. Quoted in Heylin. *Babylon's Burning*, p. 579.

54. Stephen Thomas Erlewine. "Zen Arcade," AllMusic, http://allmusic .com/album/zen-arcade-r41102 /review, 2011.

55. Stephen Thomas Erlewine. "Hüsker Dü," AllMusic, http://allmusic.com /artist/hsker-d-p4532/biography, 2011.

56. Greil Marcus. *Ranters & Crowd Pleasers*. New York: Doubleday, 1993, p. 354.

57. Quoted in Chris Campion. *Walking on the Moon*. Hoboken: John Wiley & Sons, 2010, p. 160.

58. Quoted in Campion. *Walking on the Moon*, p. 159.

59. Quoted in Simon Reynolds. *Rip It Up and Start Again*. New York: Penguin Books, 2005, p. 158.

60. Quoted in Reynolds. *Rip It Up*, p. 340.

61. Quoted in Campion. *Walking on the Moon*, p. 83.

62. Quoted in Waksman. *This Ain't the Summer of Love*, p. 167.

63. Quoted in Scott Plagenhoef and Ryan Schreiber. *The Pitchfork 500*. New York: Simon & Schuster, 2008, p. 57.

64. Wendy Fonarow. *Empire of Dirt*.

Middletown, CT: Wesleyan University Press, 2006, p. 51.

Chapter 4: The Golden Age of Grunge

65. Lester Bangs. *Psychotic Reactions and Carburetor Dung*. New York: Vintage Books, 1988, p. 102.

66. Quoted in Will Hermes and Sia Michel, eds. *Spin: 20 Years of Alternative Music*. New York: Three Rivers Press, 2005, p. 149.

67. Quoted in Michael Azerrad. *Our Band Could Be Your Life: Scenes from the American Indie Underground, 1981–1991*. New York: Little, Brown and Company, 2001, p. 420.

68. Quoted in Greg Prato. *Grunge Is Dead*. Toronto: ECW Press, 2009, p. 160.

69. Quoted in Gillian G. Gaar. *The Rough Guide to Nirvana*. London: Rough Guides, 2009, p. 35.

70. Quoted in Michael Azerrad. "Seattle: Grunge City," *Rolling Stone*, April 16, 1992, p. 44.

71. Quoted in Plagenhoef and Schreiber. *The Pitchfork 500*, p. 102.

72. Kurt Cobain. "Suicide Note (text)," Kurt Cobain's Suicide Note, http:// kurtcobainssuicidenote.com/ kurt_cobains_suicide_note.html, 2011.

73. Quoted in Plagenhoef and Schreiber. *The Pitchfork 500*, p. 121.

74. Quoted in Hermes and Michel. *Spin*, p. 171.

75. Quoted in Hermes and Michel.

Spin, p. 172.

76. Jim DeRogatis. *Milk It!* New York: DeCapo Press, 2003, pp. 81–82.
77. Quoted in Hermes and Michel. *Spin*, p. 179.
78. Quoted in Smith. *101 Albums*, p. 231.

Chapter 5: Alt-Rock's Digital New Age

79. Quoted in Hermes and Michel. *Spin*, p. 235.
80. Hermes and Michel. *Spin*, p. 213.
81. Quoted in Hermes and Michel. *Spin*, p. 235.
82. Brian Hiatt, Liane Bonin, and Karen Valby. "The Return of (Good) Alt-Rock," EW.com, www.ew.com/ew/article/0,,659881,00.html, July 9, 2004.
83. Craig McLean. "Yeah Yeah Yeahs: Why Fans of the Art-Punk Trio Can't Say No," Times Online, http://entertainment.timesonline.co.uk/tol/arts_and_entertainment/music/article6485717.ece, June 13, 2009.
84. David Marchese. "Who Cares About Creed's Comeback?" *Spin*, http://new.music.yahoo.com/blogs/spin/5975/who-cares-about-creeds-comeback/?page=2, May 4, 2009.
85. Quoted in Hiatt, Bonin, and Valby. "The Return of (Good) Alt-Rock."
86. Quoted in Melinda Newman. "Retail's View of Branded CD-Rs," *Billboard*, October 9, 2004, p. 67.
87. Quoted in Smith. *101 Albums*, p. 227.
88. Diehl. *My So-Called Punk*, p. 19.
89. Ben Meyers. *Green Day: American Idiots & The New Punk Explosion*. New York: The Disinformation Company, 2006, p. 196.
90. Quoted in Meyers. *Green Day*, p. 196.
91. Quoted in Meyers. *Green Day*, p. 202.
92. Quoted in Diehl. *My So-Called Punk*, p. 7.
93. Quoted in Plagenhoef and Schreiber. *The Pitchfork 500*, p. 190.
94. Quoted in Plagenhoef and Schreiber. *The Pitchfork 500*, p. 191.
95. Ian Cohen. "Arcade Fire: The Suburbs," Pitchfork, www.pitchfork.com/reviews/albums/14516-the-suburbs, August 2, 2010.

AC/DC

Dirty Deeds Done Dirt Cheap, 1976

This album helped the Australian heavy metal headbangers attract a large British punk audience, influenced a generation of New Wave of British Heavy Metal, or NWOBHM, bands, and led the group to international success.

Highway to Hell, 1979

The Razor's Edge, 1990

Arcade Fire

Funeral, 2004

Neon Bible, 2007

Recorded in a church the band was renovating, Arcade Fire's breakout album is a symphonic masterpiece of clamor rock, with rich, warped, desperate textures filled out with cello, harp, viola, brass, and choir arrangements.

The Suburbs, 2010

Beatles

The Beatles, 1968

Some of the thirty songs on this record, also known as *The White Album*, could be considered the first alternative music, spanning a range of styles from surf music, noise collages, and ironic folk songs to heavy metal and proto-punk.

Beck

Odelay, 1996

Mutations, 1998

Midnight Vultures, 1999

Clash

London Calling, 1980

Punk rock injected with politics and played by real musicians, this double album, which draws from rockabilly, R&B, hard rock, and pop influences, was the first punk record to break into the Top 40 in America.

Elvis Costello

My Aim Is True, 1977

Dashboard Confessional

The Places You Have Come to Fear the Most, 2001

With songs of love and loss from Chris Carrabba, one of the leading lights of emo, this is the album that helped bring the sound of angst and anguish to a wide audience.

***Alter the Ending*, 2009**

Bob Dylan

***Bringing It All Back Home*, 1965**

***Highway 61 Revisited*, 1965**

This album exemplifies the raw, sardonic feel of alternative rock with minimal production values, a jingle-jangle sound, and the ire, bile, and sneer of America's premier social critic calling out hucksters, hipsters, and Mr. Jones, the clueless everyman.

Foo Fighters

***Foo Fighters*, 1995**

A week after Nirvana broke up, drummer Dave Grohl invented the post-grunge sound alone at home, playing every instrument himself on an album filled with songs that might be defined as Nirvana light.

***Wasting Light*, 2011**

Green Day

***Dookie*, 1994**

Green Day's third album was their biggest success to date, and the one that made the group international stars. The hit singles from this record, including "Longview," "Welcome to Paradise," "Basket Case," and "When I Come Around," are credited with reviving punk rock for a new generation.

***American Idiot*, 2004**

***21st Century Breakdown*, 2009**

Jimi Hendrix

***Are You Experienced*, 1967**

One of only three albums Hendrix recorded with the Experience before his tragic death, this debut almost single-handedly created heavy metal with distortion, feedback, wah-wah, and fuzz tone guitar."

Hüsker Dü

***Zen Arcade*, 1984**

Iggy and the Stooges

***Raw Power*, 1973**

Jimmy Eat World

***Clarity*, 1999**

***Bleed American*, 2001**

This critically acclaimed album sold thirty thousand copies in its first week and went platinum in 2002 as the emo style broke into the mainstream.

Metallica

***Kill 'em All*, 1983**

Motorhead

***Overkill*, 1979**

This record melds heavy metal and punk rock into a ferocious thrash metal masterpiece that put maniacal metal at the top of the charts for the first time.

New York Dolls

The New York Dolls, 1973

Released during an era of platinum-selling smooth progressive rock, sincere singer-songwriters, and slick country rock, this album by a group of amateurs dressed in drag is a careening, screeching proto-punk masterpiece that inspired generations of indie rockers.

Nine Inch Nails

Pretty Hate Machine, 1989

Nirvana

Nevermind, 1991

The album that made Kurt Cobain an icon and celebrity and likely led to his suicide, this collection of angry words and sludgy guitars features the grunge anthem "Smells Like Teen Spirit."

Pearl Jam

Ten, 1991

Radiohead

OK Computer, 1997

Radiohead's first platinum album marked the band's entry into the realm of rock stardom. Ironically, the band relies on heavy electronica and computerized effects to explore the theme that technology is strangling the human spirit.

In Rainbows, 2007

Ramones

Ramones, 1976

This album joined the Kinks' fuzz tones, the Velvet Underground's minimalism, Iggy Pop's anger, and the New York Dolls' raw sound into a punk magnum opus.

Red Hot Chili Peppers

Blood Sugar Sex Magik, 1991

Californication, 1999

Lou Reed

Transformer, 1972

R.E.M.

Murmur, 1983

Document, 1987

Sex Pistols

Never Mind the Bollocks, Here's the Sex Pistols, 1977

Patti Smith

Horses, 1975

Patti Smith is the punk rock poet laureate and the first CBGB alumnus to land a major record contract. This album demonstrates how an anti-rock star can connect evocative poetry to intense no-holds-barred rock rampages and create music that is as timeless as it is influential.

Sonic Youth

Daydream Nation, 1988

Sonic Youth was the quintessential underground indie band until this album brought them stardom. The songs combine heavy metal, dance pop, hard core, sound effects, thrash, and quirky pop into an alternative soundscape that inspired the Seattle sound.

Sunny Day Real Estate

Dairy, 1994

In the debut album from the band that pioneered the emo sound, lead vocalist Jeremy Enigk sings with conviction and an overwrought sense of drama.

Sunny Day Real Estate, 1994

U2

The Joshua Tree, 1987

Pop, 1997

Vampire Weekend

Vampire Weekend, 2008

Vampire Weekend's eponymous album produced several popular singles with the band's trademark blend of sophisticated melodies, dance pop, and Afro pop.

Contra, 2010

Various Artists

Garage Rock Classics, 2010

This compilation, available only on iTunes, is filled with the songs by the Seeds, the Swingin' Medallions, and the Kingsmen that laid down the foundations for punk and grunge.

Nuggets: Original Artyfacts from the First Psychedelic Era, 1965–1968, 1998

With four CDs, this musical nugget presents a profusion of mid-sixties proto-punk garage band one-hit wonders like the Standells' "Dirty Water," Music Machine's "Talk Talk," and the Hombres' "Let It Out (Let It All Hang Out)."

Velvet Underground

The Velvet Underground and Nico, 1967

This album influenced a generation of punk and new-wave musicians and provided a dark, brooding alternative to the psychedelic rock of the era.

White Light/White Heat, 1968

GLOSSARY

album: Originally used to describe a 12-inch (30cm) vinyl, long-playing (LP) record that played at 33 rpm (revolutions per minute) and could hold about twenty minutes of music on each side. In the digital age, an album is any collection of songs released together by an artist.

chord: A set of notes played simultaneously, as on a guitar or piano. Chords in a major key provide a joyful sound, while chords in a minor key are moody and blue.

hook: A memorable melody that catches, or hooks, the listener's attention.

improvising: The act of composing music while playing it, also known as jamming.

multi-instrumentalist: A person who is proficient on more than one instrument.

one-hit wonder: A group that tops the charts with one song and never has another hit.

platinum: A term used to describe records that sell more than 1 million copies. Multiplatinum records sell more than 2 million copies.

proto-punk: *Proto-* means earliest, and *proto-punk* is a term used to describe the music of the 1960s and early 1970s that influenced the punk rock movement, which began around 1975.

psychedelic: A word used to describe the hallucinatory effects of the drug LSD (lysergic acid diethylamide, or acid), from Greek words that mean "to manifest the soul."

sampling: The technique of pasting together short sound segments from earlier recordings to form a new sound. Sampling is very popular with hip-hop and alternative rock artists.

single: Originally any record with a single song on each side. In the 1950s, singles were sold as 7-inch (17.7cm) vinyl records that played at 45 rpm (revolutions per minute). In the digital age, a single is any one song that is promoted separately from an album.

synthesizer: An electronic instrument, usually played with a keyboard, that produces unique complex sounds or those that mimic other instruments such as violins and horns.

vinyl: Short for polyvinyl chloride, the material used to make 7-inch (17.7cm) singles and 12-inch (30cm) long-playing (LP) albums.

Books

Jeff Burlingame. *Kurt Cobain: Oh Well, Whatever, Nevermind*. Berkeley Heights, NJ: Enslow, 2007. The inside story of Nirvana's front man, written by one of his high school acquaintances. The book includes interviews with Cobain's friends and family members and describes his shining musical genius along with his dark struggles with drugs and depression.

Editors of *Rolling Stone*. *The '90s: The Inside Stories from the Decade That Rocked*. New York: Harper Design, 2010. Fifty stories and dozens of photographs from the decade that produced indie, grunge, gangsta rap, and teen pop. Articles cover Pearl Jam, Eminem, Dave Matthews, Guns N' Roses, Nirvana, U2, and others.

Noa Flynn. *The Who*. Broomall, PA: Mason Crest, 2008. This book covers the formation of the Who, its rise to stardom, and the difficulties the band faced during key moments in their career.

Kenneth McIntosh. *The Grateful Dead*. Broomall, PA: Mason Crest, 2008. Between 1965 and 1996, the Dead was one of the leading do-it-yourself bands. This book explores the group's unique sound and unusual path to success.

Kenneth McIntosh. *U2*. Broomall, PA: Mason Crest, 2008. The story of Bono and the boys, how the group developed its alt-rock sound, and the impact of U2 on modern alt-rock.

Wendy S. Mead. *The Alternative Rock Scene: The Stars, the Fans, the Music*. Berkeley Heights, NJ: Enslow, 2009. This book covers the alt-rock scene from indie and grunge to goth and punk, exploring the music, fans, clothes, concerts, and stars of alternative culture.

Heather Miller. *The Rolling Stones: The Greatest Rock Band*. Berkeley Heights, NJ: Enslow, 2010. This book profiles each band member, discusses their collective fascination with American blues music, and follows the Stones from early sixties London to the twenty-first century.

Craig Morrison and Thom Holmes. *American Popular Music: Rock and Roll*. New York: Facts On File, 2012. This book covers the story of rock-and-roll music with in-depth coverage of the early days, its amazing growth in the sixties and seventies, and the rock and roll of the twenty-first century.

Travis Nichols. *Punk Rock Etiquette: The Ultimate How-to Guide for DIY, Punk, Indie, and Underground Bands*. New York: Macmillan, 2008. Although this irreverent book is aimed at those wishing to start their own band, it is full of fun facts and humorous cartoons covering indie life, attitude, and culture.

Scott Plagenhoef and Ryan Schreiber, eds. *The Pitchfork 500: Our Guide to the Greatest Songs from Punk to the Present*. New York: Simon & Schuster, 2008. This book, from the creators of the alt-rock Pitchfork website, is a guide to the greatest songs of punk, hard core, grunge, indie, and other styles around since 1977. Although the book ends in 2007, it has a broad scope and is filled with insightful reviews of songs as well as trends in alternative music, business, and culture.

Greg Prato. *Grunge Is Dead*. Toronto: ECW Press, 2009. An oral history of the Seattle sound in the 1980s and 1990s through the eyes and ears of those who witnessed the rise of Nirvana, Pearl Jam, and others.

Randi Reisfeld. *This Is the Sound: The Best of Alternative Rock*. New York: Simon Pulse, 2011. Nine alt-rock acts are profiled in this book, including Green Day, Nine Inch Nails, Hole, and the Cranberries. Each chapter begins with a short passage about how the band got its name, followed by musical details, influences, and band contact information.

Jeremy Roberts. *The Beatles: Music Revolutionaries*. Minneapolis: Twenty-First Century Books, 2011. This book covers the Beatles from the group's formation in Liverpool, England, through their journey to the international stage as the most popular rock group in history.

Debra Wolter, ed. *Punk: The Whole Story*. London: DK, 2006. This book covers the punk rock movement from a British perspective with interviews, dazzling photos, and articles taken from the archives of the U.K. music magazine *Mojo*. Chapters follow the Ramones, Blondie, the Sex Pistols, and others through their revolutionary musical escapades.

Internet

AllMusic (www.allmusic.com). Originally known as All Music Guide (AMG), the AllMusic website is one of the most comprehensive music guides on the Internet. The site has in-depth information about old music, classics, and the latest hits as well as descriptions of genres from opera to punk.

MTV (www.mtv.com). The homepage of MTV features music news, artist biographies, fashions, and thousands of videos from the 1980s to the present.

Pitchfork (www.pitchfork.com). Founded in 1995 and updated daily, Pitchfork focuses on criticism, commentary, and news concerning new music, especially underground and indie rock. The site is credited for breaking artists such as Arcade Fire and Modest Mouse.

Rolling Stone (www.rollingstone.com). *Rolling Stone* has been covering pop stars and the music industry since the 1960s. The magazine's website contains the latest music and pop culture news, biographies of everyone from Jimmie Rodgers to Blink-182, and music, movie, and video reviews and downloads.

Films

Bullet in a Bible, 2005
This film documents the two biggest shows Green Day ever headlined, when they played to more than 130,000 people over the course of two days in the United Kingdom.

Frank Zappa: Does Humor Belong in Music?, 1985
Zappa performs live in concert with some of the best musicians of the day, playing head-spinning orchestrated rock music unlike any written before or since.

Hype, 1996
This documentary about the Seattle music scene features performances by Nirvana, Pearl Jam, and others and captures a moment in time when grunge exploded out of basements and garages into a pop culture phenomenon.

Stop Making Sense, 1984
Critic Leonard Maltin called this film, of the Talking Heads playing live in their funk punk prime, the greatest rock movie ever made.

The Decline of Western Civilization, 1981
This music-driven documentary about the hard-hitting early 1980s Los Angeles punk scene includes live performances by Black Flag, the Germs, X, the Bags, and Fear, plus interviews with the bands and the extreme fans who love them.

The Filth and the Fury, 2000
This film covers the short career of the Sex Pistols and features elements of the social, political, and musical scene in Britain that helped launch the punk rock movement.

INDEX

S

Sampling, 82, 84–85, 98
Scream (band), 72
Selway, Phil, 88
Sex Pistols, 15, 43–48, *44*, 50, 59, 95
Shocking Blue, 70
Silverchair, 78
Simonon, Paul, 43, 50–51
Siouxie and the Banshees, 48
60ft Dolls, 28
Ska, 49, 51–52
Smashing Pumpkins, 13, 79, *80*, 84
Smith, Patti, 38, 40–42, *41*, 47
Sonic Youth, 75
Sonics (band), 39, 68
Soul Asylum, 56
Soundgarden, 28, 68, 69, 73, 74, 76
Spears, Britney, 90
Speed metal, 62
Springsteen, Bruce, 13
Stein, Chris, 40
Sting, 60, *61*
Stipe, Michael, 64, *65*
Stooges, 12, 15, 35–38
Strokes (band), 92, 99
Strummer, Joe, 50–51
Suicidal Tendencies, 55
Summers, Andy, 60
Sunny Day Real Estate, 102
Superchunk, 57

T

Talking Heads, 58–61, *59*
Taylor, Phil "Philthy Animal," 62
Tears for Fears, 58
Television (band), 39–40, *39*, 42, 44, 59
Thayil, Kim, 74
Them (band), 15, 39
Thompson Twins, 58
Thrash, 6, 53, 61–63, 75, 87

Timbaland, 99
Tool, 75
Toots and the Maytals, 13
Townshend, Pete, 19
Tré Cool, 94–95
A Tribe Called Quest, 75
Tucker, Maureen "Mo," 33–34, *33*, 90

U

U2, *8*, 22, 24, 34, 82, 84, 101
Ulrich, Lars, 87
Umphrey's McGee, 26

V

Vampire Weekend, 10
Van Halen, 62
Vedder, Eddie, *74*
Velvet Underground, 31–34, 36, 38, 39, 43, 90
Verlaine, Tom (Tom Miller), 39
Vicious, Sid, 43, *44*, 48

W

Wah-wah pedal, 74
Weir, Bob, *25*
Weymouth, Tina, 59, *59*
White, Jack, 89–92, *90*
White, Meg, 90, *90*
White Stripes, 89–92, *90*, 99
The Who, 15, 17, 18, *19*, 20
Wretzky, D'arcy, 79

Y

Yeah Yeah Yeahs, 92–93
Yorke, Thom, 88, *88*

Z

Zappa, Frank, 12, 13, 29, *29*

PICTURE CREDITS

ABOUT THE AUTHOR

Stuart A. Kallen is the author of more than 250 nonfiction books for children and young adults. He has written extensively about science, the environment, music, culture, history, and folklore. In addition, Mr. Kallen has written award-winning children's videos and television scripts. In his spare time, he is a singer/songwriter/guitarist in San Diego, California.